THE SMITHSONIAN ILLUSTRATED LIBRARY OF ANTIQUES

General Editor: Brenda Gilchrist

Glass

Paul Vickers Gardner

COOPER-HEWITT MUSEUM

The Smithsonian Institution's National Museum of Design

ENDPAPERS
Drawings of German drinking glasses showing designs for
applied decorations. Detail of a page from a sketchbook
published in Stuttgart in 1897. Picture Collection, Cooper-
Hewitt Museum Library

FRONTISPIECE
One of a pair of cut-glass candelabra on a Wedgwood jasper-
ware base with gilt-bronze mountings. England, c. 1785.
Height: 104.2 cm. (41 in.). Cooper-Hewitt Museum, gift
of Irwin Untermyer

Art Direction, Design: JOSEPH B. DEL VALLE

Text Editor: JOAN HOFFMAN

Picture Editor: LISA LITTLE

Contents

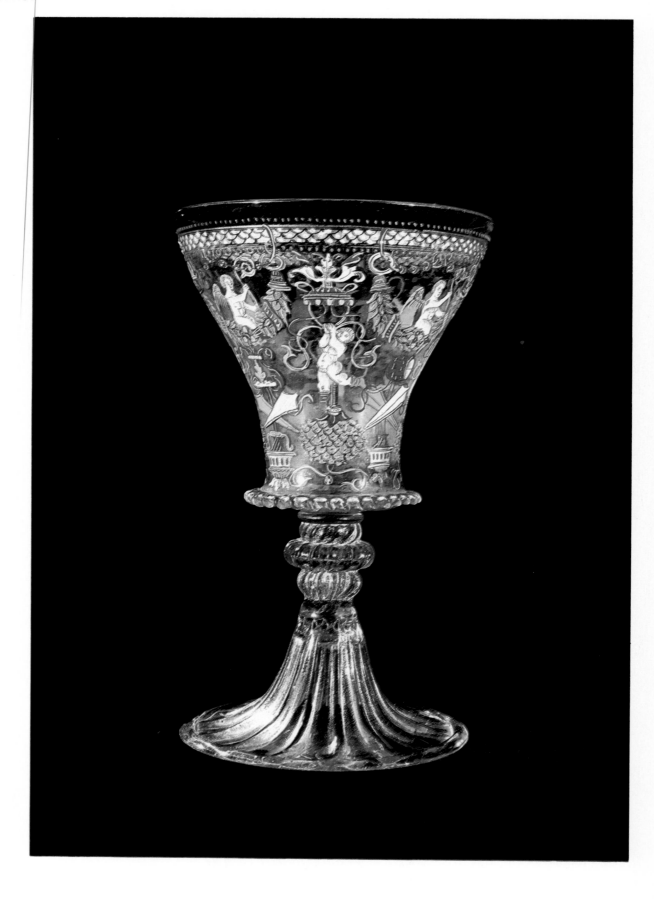

Introduction

This book traces the history of ornamental and useful glass production from antiquity to the World War I years of 1914–18 and touches upon a few of the important developments occurring later in the twentieth century. The first part of the book, following a brief look at the techniques of glassmaking, deals with the Near East and Europe and presents chronologically, as far as practicable, some of the most significant contributions of the area's various cultures and periods, beginning in the second and first millennia B.C. This was the remarkable era of the Mesopotamian and Egyptian artisans. They were followed by the great Roman glassmakers, who dominated the period from about the first century B.C. to the fifth century A.D. After Rome fell, the leadership in glassmaking shifted to the Islamic centers, remaining there from about the sixth to the fourteenth century. With the rise of the Venetian industry in the thirteenth and fourteenth centuries, the domination returned to the West, and by the fifteenth century Venetian supremacy in glassmaking was firmly established. The Italian influence made itself felt throughout continental Europe in the sixteenth and seventeenth centuries; then came the rise of the powerful German, Bohemian, French and Spanish centers. Other central and western European centers, including those in England and Ireland, also made contributions to the industry.

The second part of the book deals with the New World and tells of the early struggles of glassmakers in Virginia and southern New Jersey; of the spread of the industry to Pennsylvania, Maryland and New York; and of the rise of the important Midwestern and New England factories. The phenomenal growth of the industry during the nineteenth century is highlighted, with references to the persons and factories contributing to this development. The decline of glassmaking at the end of the nineteenth century and its rejuvenation in the early twentieth are noted, concluding with a glance at the Studio Glass Movement and prospects for the future of artistic glass.

Colorplate 1.
An exquisite free-blown *cristallo* goblet with painted enamel decorations made by Venetian artists as a presentation piece. Venice, early sixteenth century. Height: 23.6 cm. (9¼ in.). Corning Museum of Glass, Corning, N.Y.

The author hopes that this book will increase the reader's interest and pleasure in glass and encourage further study of collections and relevant books, particularly in those fields that could not be adequately covered in the limited space available. Regrettably, many specializations had to be given scant attention or even omitted. In the Reading and Reference section at the back of the book, collectors will find a listing of fine books that may be consulted for detailed information on almost any aspect of glassmaking in which they have an interest.

Nineteenth-century blowing-room interior showing (far left) glassblowers drawing a length of glass tubing above the rack where it will be placed when finished; (background) glassblower marvering a gather of molten glass and two others gathering from the glass furnace; (foreground) the gaffer, or head glassblower, shaping an object while seated in the glassmaker's "chair" and two glassblowers blowing and forming the molten glass. Print from a nineteenth-century German book (unidentified). Kubler Collection 3225, Picture Collection, Cooper-Hewitt Museum Library

1 Techniques of Glassmaking

Glass is such a beautiful and versatile material that it is hard to believe it can be made by simply melting sand with the proper amounts of soda and lime. Its glowing colors are obtained by adding cobalt, iron or other metallic oxides to the basic ingredients. For more than thirty-five hundred years glass has satisfied man's wish for luxury objects and met his need for everyday articles and scientific equipment. The fragility of glass is part of its charm, yet when gently handled glass also has great durability. For example, some delicate glass objects made almost thirty-five hundred years ago exist today in mint condition.

Formulas for most standard types of glass are now well known, but until it became possible to analyze glass these formulas were carefully guarded. Even now there are many refinements and trade secrets which glassmakers keep to themselves.

The most common type of glass, which has been made since ancient times, is *soda-lime glass*. Its melting temperature is about 1500 degrees Celsius. *Lead-crystal glass*, also called *flint glass*, is a brilliant, resonant glass containing up to one-third lead oxide in the batch (mixture of ingredients). Perfected in England about 1676, it has been used since for high-quality decorative objects and tablewares. Its melting temperature is about 1400 degrees Celsius. *Borosilicate glass* contains about twelve percent boron oxide, which is added to the batch to lower the coefficient of expansion and make a heat-resistant glass for baking wares and scientific uses. The melting temperature of borosilicate glass is about 1600 degrees Celsius.

Although fuels have changed and tools and processes have evolved and blowing-room layouts have been adapted to special needs, glassmaking factories have continued to use somewhat similar basic arrangements and equipment for centuries. The manufacturing processes have also remained standard, particularly where hand-blown objects are concerned. Basically, glass objects are formed by free-blowing,

Nineteenth-century blowing-room interior showing glassblowers forming a free-blown vase. Left to right: expanding the parison by blowing; further shaping of the glass bubble; forming of the vase by the gaffer, or head glassblower (seated in the glassmaker's "chair"), with the assistance of an apprentice. Print from a nineteenth-century German book (unidentified). Kubler Collection 3225, Picture Collection, Cooper-Hewitt Museum Library

Blowing room in a flat (window) glass factory showing processes in making window and plate glass. Workmen around furnace at left are blowing and forming a crown glass disk: (C) glassblower shapes parison on marver; (D) glassblower expands glass bubble; (E) glassblower reheats disk prior to final expansion. The operation at right shows workmen (P) spreading molten glass (O) from an iron container (K) on a metal table (N) prior to its being rolled into a sheet of plate glass by workman holding roller (Q). In background workman (A) uses a sledge to smash cullet, which will be added to the glass batch during the melting process. A notice at the bottom of this eighteenth-century engraving reads, "Printed for J. Hinton at the Kings Arms in St. Pauls Church Yard London—For the *Universal Magazine*, November 1747." Kubler Collection 4329, Picture Collection, Cooper-Hewitt Museum Library

mold-blowing and mold-pressing, or by combinations of these processes. In *free-blowing* the object is formed by hand with the assistance of the basic hand tools and other equipment of glassblowers. The blowing iron (blowpipe) is used to gather the glass from the glass pot and to blow the basic bubble (parison), which is then shaped with simple tools in a series of basic steps. *Mold-blowing* is done by blowing the parison into a full-size mold, which can be plain or have a pattern cut or molded on the inner surface. In pattern-molding, the forming of the glass is begun by inserting the parison in a mold having ribs, diamonds or other pattern and expanding the parison sufficiently in the mold to impress the pattern on the hot glass bubble. This patterned parison is then removed from the mold and expanded to the full-size object, giving a larger and softer version of the molded pattern to the finished piece. *Mold-pressing* is accomplished by placing a gather of hot glass in a mold and pressing it into the desired form with a plunger.

For centuries flat glass (window and sheet glass) was made by either the crown glass or the cylinder glass (also called muff and broad glass) method. In the *crown glass method* a blown bubble of glass is expanded and transferred from the blowing iron to the pontil rod. The bubble is then opened and flared out by centrifugal force to form a disk usually averaging from three to five feet in diameter. After this disk is broken from the pontil, leaving a bull's-eye in the center, it is annealed and cut into panes. In the *cylinder* (or *broad*) *glass method*, the glassmaker blows a cylinder of glass about a foot in diameter and three to five feet long, beginning the process in a mold. After removal from the blowing iron, the ends of the cylinder are cut off and a vertical cut in one side allows the cylinder to open and become flat when heated in a flattening oven. After annealing, this large flat sheet is cut into the desired sizes.

2 Glass from the Pharaohs to the Sultans

The jewel-like qualities of glass have always tempted craftsmen to use it as a substitute for gems and semiprecious stones. Glass inlays ornamented Tutankhamun's celebrated gold mask as well as his falcon pectoral necklace and vulture collar and the miniature coffins and alabaster vases found in his tomb. Emerald green, amethyst and alabaster white glass vessels have frequently been mistaken for objects made from the precious materials they resemble. Marbleized glasses also were made at least as early as the first century B.C. and have continued to be produced in many variations to the present day.

Although glass vessels were made in western Asia early in the second millennium B.C., the earliest glass pieces which have been positively dated are three small vessels bearing the cartouche of the pharaoh Thutmose III (c. 1504–1450 B.C.). One of these, a jug, is in the British Museum, London; another, a goblet, is in the Antike Abteilung, Munich; and the third, an elegant goblet which is the most impressive of the three, is in the Metropolitan Museum of Art, New York (plate 1).

From the fifteenth century B.C. until the beginning of the Christian Era, all glass objects were luxury items and could be produced only by laborious and time-consuming processes. The best known of these processes, and the one of which the most examples have been preserved, was *core-forming*. In this technique a core, probably of clay and dung, was shaped in the general form of the object and attached to the end of a metal rod. It was then covered with a coating of glass, usually by winding threads of hot glass around it, or by dipping it in a pot of molten glass. When the glass coating reached the desired thickness, it was shaped and smoothed by rolling it over a flat surface (a process called *marvering* today), usually with frequent reheatings. After cooling, the core was removed. These core-formed vessels were limited in size and shape. Egyptian pieces (colorplate 2) are generally

Colorplate 2.
These luxury glass flasks may have graced the dressing table of an elegant Egyptian lady more than three thousand years ago. All are core-formed, and two have applied hooked (dragged) decoration. Egypt, 1400–1250 B.C. Height of tallest flask: 12.7 cm. (5 in.). Corning Museum of Glass, Corning, N.Y.

not over eight inches in height, but a few measuring up to fourteen inches, possibly not made in Egypt, have been found in Egyptian tombs. These vessels were often decorated by trailing threads of hot glass in radiating or horizontal patterns around part or all of the body of the object, a process called *trailing* or *threading*. Often these threads were pulled up and down with a hook-shaped tool while hot to form wavy or chevron patterns. This manipulation produced what is now called a *hooked*, or *dragged*, pattern (plate 3). After the discovery of glassblowing in about 50 B.C., core-forming died out altogether.

Massive cutting and lathe-turning to form glass objects from glass blocks or ingots were other techniques practiced in Egypt at least as early as the fifteenth century B.C. A process now called *pâte de verre* (glass paste) was also introduced during this period. Powdered glass was fused in molds to produce vessels, bas-relief plaques and small sculptures as well as the miniature masks often used as inlays in furniture or decorative objects (plate 2).

Beaker fragments found in Iraq and adjacent areas show that the *fused mosaic method* of glassmaking was used in this region as early as the fifteenth century B.C. As the name suggests, fused mosaic glass was made by placing sections of glass rods, bits of glass or combinations of these elements in molds in a variety of mosaiclike designs and fusing them together. After cooling, these objects were ground and polished to give them their final form. The process was used intermittently throughout the first millennium B.C. and by the third century B.C. had become much more advanced (plate 4). Later Egyptian and Roman artisans continued the technique, refining it further from the first century B.C. on. When Venetian glassmakers revived the process during the Renaissance, they called the glass *millefiori* (thousand flowers).

Even though Egyptian and Mesopotamian glassmakers of the second and first millennia B.C. were limited in their techniques and colors, they have left a heritage of beautiful luxury glass objects and some fundamental glassmaking concepts which have continued to be exploited by artisans to the present day.

The Roman Empire   The discovery of glassblowing during the first century B.C., probably in Phoenicia or Syria, revolutionized the glassmaking industry. From then on glass pieces could be made so much more easily and quickly that both useful and decorative objects became available to nearly everyone. Coinciding as it did with the beginning of the Roman Empire toward the end of the first century B.C., the invention of the glassblowing tube, or blowpipe, gave great impetus to the development of the glass industry in the regions coming under Roman domination from about the first to the fifth century A.D. Regardless of where in the empire it was produced, glass made during this period is now called Roman glass.

1.
Handsome goblet in turquoise blue glass made for the pharaoh Thutmose III and incised with his cartouche and lotus motifs. One of the earliest dated glass pieces known. Egypt, Eighteenth Dynasty, c. 1490 B.C. Height: 13.1 cm. (5⅛ in.). Metropolitan Museum of Art, New York, bequest of Lord Carnarvon, 1923

2.
Miniature mask cast in opaque blue glass by the *pâte de verre* process. After cooling, the facial details were heightened by carving. Back and top of head have been flattened and formed into a rectangular peg. Probably used as an ornamental inlay. Egypt, Eighteenth Dynasty (c. 1570–1293 B.C.). Height: 5.7 cm. (2¼ in.). Smithsonian Institution, National Collection of Fine Arts, gift of John Gellatly

3.
Columnar flask with palm-shaped capital made to contain kohl (an eye makeup). Core-formed of turquoise blue glass with hooked (dragged) decoration in yellow and white. Egypt, Eighteenth Dynasty (c. 1570–1293 B.C.). Height: 11.2 cm. (4⅜ in.). Smithsonian Institution, National Collection of Fine Arts, gift of John Gellatly

4.
Fused mosaic glass dish made in a pattern composed of sections cut from glass canes and fused together in a mold. The sections containing a white spiral with a yellow center were cut from the same rod and interspersed with gold and yellow glass tesserae. Italy, Canosa, Apulia, late third century B.C. Diameter: 30.8 cm. (12⅛ in.). British Museum, London

1

2

3

4

5.
The Portland Vase (also called the Barberini Vase) is one of the most famous pieces of Roman cameo glass. Blown of dark blue glass cased with opaque white and cut and carved in cameo style with figures depicting Thetis reclining between Hermes and Aphrodite. Roman Empire, late first century B.C. or early first century A.D. Height: 24 cm. (9½ in.). British Museum, London

Roman artisans discovered and practiced all the basic glassmaking techniques in use today, with the exception of machine production and the highly specialized processes made possible by the advanced glass technology of the twentieth century. Thus they took the industry from a relatively minor craft producing a limited number of luxury items to a national industry with untold influence on every glassmaking center up to the present day.

As Roman glassmakers became proficient in glassblowing, they continued to produce luxury glass which rivaled or excelled that made in any other era. One of their first outstanding accomplishments was mastering the complicated technique of making *cameo glass* (colorplate 3). In making cameo glass it is necessary to case (or cover) glass of one color with an outer layer of glass of another color. The formulas

Colorplate 3.
The carved cameo glass bowl, miniature torso of Aphrodite and pyxis (covered jar) in marbled glass with gold veinings, called gold-band glass, show the mastery of these techniques by Roman artists of the first to second centuries A.D. Height of torso: 9.5 cm. (3¾ in.). Corning Museum of Glass, Corning, N.Y.

of both glasses must be compatible so that when the two layers are fused together, both will have the same coefficient of expansion. If one layer expands or contracts more than the other, the glass will crack or literally fly to pieces as soon as it starts to cool. Since glassmakers as late as the nineteenth century had difficulties with this process, it is amazing that the ancients were able to produce such complex pieces. Symbolizing this great Roman achievement is the world-famous Portland Vase, which dates from the late first century B.C. or the early first century A.D. (plate 5).

Roman artisans continued to make fused mosaic glass, using variations of the ancient techniques. Besides exquisite bowls (colorplate 4), they produced many small panels and medallions, which often were used as inlays, in designs ranging from animals and human heads to floral friezes (plate 6).

From time to time connoisseurs have thought some of the fine jewel-like bowls and other pieces might be the rare *vasa murrhina* objects mentioned by Pliny and other classical authors. Interest in these fabulous luxury pieces has been heightened because a number of important historical personages have legendary connections with them. A murrhine cup from Cleopatra's collection is supposed to have been sold in Rome for a sum equal to fifty times the annual pay of a Roman legionnaire. Pompey was reputed to have brought murrhine pieces back to Rome after he conquered Mithridates and to have dedicated them to Jupiter. Even Nero is said to have paid a huge sum for a murrhine drinking vessel. Since the material of murrhine objects was not described in the ancient writings, considerable research has been undertaken in an attempt to determine if it was glass. The latest findings indicate the pieces were probably made from semiprecious stones or minerals, such as fluorspar, rather than glass. There is always the possibility that enterprising glassmakers deliberately made glass imita-

Colorplate 4.
Jewel-like bowls of fused mosaic glass were highly prized by affluent Romans in the early Christian Era. The bowl (or beaker) on the left is now called ribbon glass. Roman Empire, all possibly Alexandria, Egypt, first century B.C.–first century A.D. Diameter of center bowl: 13.4 cm. (5¼ in.). Corning Museum of Glass, Corning, N.Y.

6.
Fused mosaic glass panel with a frieze of lotus motifs in blue, white and greenish blue on an opaque red ground. Perhaps used as an ornamental inlay. Roman Empire, Egypt, first century B.C.–first century A.D. Length: 5.8 cm. (2¼ in.). Smithsonian Institution, National Museum of History and Technology

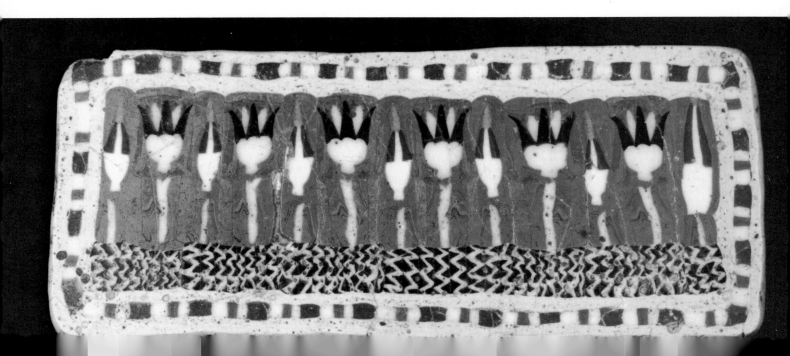

tions of the celebrated objects, perhaps in admiration of their beauty, but perhaps with the less laudable hope that the imitations would be mistaken for the true *vasa murrhina*.

A Roman luxury glass which has no mystery concerning its materials but which nevertheless has rarely been duplicated is *fondi d'oro* (gold glass). In making this type of glass, designs in gold leaf were enclosed between two layers of transparent glass, which were then fused together. Variations of this technique were done earlier, but the best-known examples are a series of fourth-century fragments, mostly bottoms of bowls, found in catacombs near Rome (colorplate 5). Other important fragments were excavated in Cologne, Germany. Whether the process was too difficult for later glassmakers or was lost entirely is not known, but no *fondi d'oro* seems to have been made for centuries after the Roman domination ended. A few pieces were made in the nineteenth century by Venetian artisans, and in the twentieth century American studio glassmakers produced some variations of the process.

The engraved and cut decorations found on Roman glass vary widely both in the quality of the work and in the subjects depicted. Lapidaries probably decorated much of the finer luxury glass, often with biblical or mythological subjects. Less skillful engravers depicted chariot races and gladiatorial combats. A human touch was provided by occasional pieces of common glass with local scenes and everyday events rather carelessly engraved on beakers and bottles (plate 7).

The intriguing ancient objects called *vasa diatreta*, or more correctly cage cups, made in the third or fourth century A.D., illustrate one of the rarest and most difficult decorating processes in the history of glassmaking. In this process the netlike outer layer or cage was produced by carving or grinding away most of the outer surface of a thick glass vessel, leaving a thin netlike design supported by integral pegs about an eighth of an inch above the inner wall. Fewer than twenty-five of these ancient pieces are known; all were probably made by Roman craftsmen in central Europe or Italy, although two were found in Greece. Several are round-bottomed footless beakers, or cups, ranging from about four to six inches in height. Some have a border inscription around the top, often in glass of a different color, indicating that the blank (the undecorated piece) was cased glass. The lower portion was usually covered with a network of adjoining circles (plate 8). Perhaps the largest piece in this technique is a situla (bucket) about ten inches high, now kept in the Treasury of St. Mark's, Venice. The top border of the situla is a frieze of horsemen, and the lower part is covered with a network of adjoining circles similar to those on the cups mentioned above.

Probably the most notable example of this intricate carving is the Lycurgus Cup, perhaps made in Alexandria, Egypt (or in Italy), in the fourth century A.D. and now in the British Museum. The extraor-

Colorplate 5.
Fragmentary disk (actually the bottom of a bowl embedded in plaster) having a *fondi d'oro* design depicting Christ holding wreaths over the heads of Peter and Paul. Rome, fourth century. Diameter of fragment: 9.3 cm. (3⅝ in.). Metropolitan Museum of Art, New York, Rogers Fund, 1911

7

8

9

7.
Greenish blown-glass bottle, probably a souvenir of Puteoli, a port city near Naples. The shallow engravings depict Puteoli's waterfront buildings along with their names. The top inscription reads, "Anima felix vivas," which, freely translated, means "Live a long and happy life." Roman Empire, Italy, A.D. 350–400. Height: 18.5 cm. (7¼ in.). Corning Museum of Glass, Corning, N.Y.

8.
Cage cup, or *diatreta* glass, an example of one of the rarest decorative processes in glassmaking history. Greenish blue transparent glass matrix with top inscription in red, center border in yellow orange and lower network in bluish green. Roman Empire, Germany, probably the Rhineland, fourth century A.D. Height: 12.1 cm. (4¾ in.). Museen der Stadt Köln, Römisch-Germanisches Museum, Cologne

9.
Roman everyday glass vessels, including two balsamaria. All free-blown in greenish yellow glass. Roman Empire, probably Syria, first–fourth century A.D. Height of tallest bottle: 19.4 cm. (7⅝ in.). Cooper-Hewitt Museum, all gift of Rodman Wanamaker, except second bottle from right, gift of Mrs. Leo Wallerstein

dinary beauty of the vessel lies not only in its exquisitely carved design, depicting the Lycurgus myth, but in its color, which is olive green by reflected light and purplish ruby by transmitted light. This unusual dichroic effect is the result of a small amount of colloidal gold in the glass formula.

While Roman luxury glass richly deserves its high place in world esteem, the practical vessels made for everyday needs (plate 9) are of tremendous interest and are much more easily obtained by collectors. So many of these wares have survived, almost miraculously, that for a relatively modest sum it is still possible to own a cosmetic flask or drinking vessel purchased by an ancient Roman from his local shop or favorite glassmaker almost two thousand years ago.

Most common wares were made in tones of yellow, green and aqua —colors often imparted to the glass by impurities, primarily iron, in the batch materials. Deep blues, dark and honey ambers and the rarer reds and purples were intentionally produced by the addition of coloring ingredients. Free-blown pitchers, vials, bowls and bottles often have delightful functional forms with skillfully applied threadings (plate 10). Pattern-molded, ribbed and swirled decorations are among other techniques collectors will recognize.

The "snake thread" was an innovative use of applied threading found on a group of second- and third-century flasks and droppers (sprinklers) made in Syria and Cologne, Germany. These pieces had rather heavy threads trailed over most of the surface in a meandering series of loops and spirals resembling, as the name suggests, a writhing snake. Some threadings were flattened and notched while hot and end in a triangular "head" that accentuates the snakelike effect (plate 11).

Mold-blown wares formed a large part of the Roman glassmakers' output. These ranged from small flasks shaped like a bunch of grapes (plate 12) and beakers decorated with lotus buds to hexagonal pitchers with Christian and Jewish religious symbols.

Although most glassmakers remained anonymous, several early artisans included their names and other information on their mold-blown pieces. Some of these wares, bearing maker's marks such as *Artas: Sidon* and *Buyer Remember* in Greek and Roman lettering, were made as early as the first century. One of these advertising glassmakers was Ennion, possibly a Syrian who later moved to northern Italy and worked near Venice. His mark, *Ennion made me*, or some other reminder in Greek lettering, was enclosed in a rectangular frame and incorporated into the design (plate 13). Fourteen pieces have been attributed to Ennion on the basis of his molded signatures.

The iridescence found on many ancient glass pieces (see plates 10 and 11) is the result of burial and was not on the object when used by its Roman owner. It is actually a deterioration of the glass surface caused by exposure to corrosive elements during centuries of burial. This exposure results in a microscopic honeycombing of the surface

10.   11.

10.
The brilliant blue iridescence enhancing the body of this free-blown bottle is the result of centuries of burial. A single opaque white spiral glass thread, skillfully trailed from top to bottom, encircles the bottle sixteen times and is nearly nine feet long. Roman Empire, Syria, second century A.D. Height: 15.8 cm. (6¼ in.). Smithsonian Institution, National Museum of History and Technology

11.
This greenish glass dropper has a glowing surface iridescence due to burial and an applied "snake thread" decoration. A dropper has a horizontal disk with a small hole in the center enclosed in the neck. The perforated disk allows the contents to be dispersed in drops when the user shakes the inverted bottle. Roman Empire, probably Syria, second–third century A.D. Height: 10.7 cm. (4¼ in.). Smithsonian Institution, National Museum of History and Technology

which reflects and refracts the light, producing a myriad of colors depending upon the degree of deterioration. Some ancient pieces have developed a predominantly gold or blue iridescence. These are much admired by collectors and were the inspiration for the iridescent glass created by Louis Comfort Tiffany and by Frederick Carder.

Medieval Europe   Late in the fourth century, when the barbarian invasions signaled the disintegration of the Roman Empire, glassmaking in central and western Europe deteriorated to a marked degree. Most of the sophisticated techniques practiced by the Roman artisans, such as cameo and mosaic glass, seem to have been lost. For about the next five hundred years, European glassmakers produced mostly drinking vessels in relatively simple forms. Even the glass used to produce these functional objects reverted to the more basic formulas; their greenish blues, yellows and browns were reminiscent of the colors found in the earlier common Roman wares.

During this period most French and German glasshouses were located in or near forests so that they would be close to a supply of wood for fuel. Because of these woodland locations the German name *Waldglas* (forest glass) and the French term *verre de fougère*

12

(bracken glass) have come to designate much of the medieval glass made in these countries. Although *Waldglas* and *verre de fougère* drinking vessels such as palm cups, drinking horns and cone beakers (plate 14) often seem almost primitive when compared with Roman luxury glass, they have the forthright appeal of objects designed for specific uses. Many were footless or had small button-shaped bases, reflecting contemporary drinking customs. Guests or tavern customers usually drank while standing or reclining and turned the drinking vessel upside down on a table or handed it to a servant when the beverage was consumed.

One of the most striking medieval forms is the claw beaker the Germans called *Rüsselbecher* (literally, "trunk beaker") because the hollow projections around the sides of the glass resembled elephants' trunks (plate 15). What may have inspired this wild form must be left to the imagination, but it was perhaps the harbinger of the spectacular drinking glasses the German craftsmen would develop about a thousand years later. While medieval glassmakers did not contribute new processes or provide elegant luxury wares, their forest factories kept the craft alive and formed a basis for its rejuvenation in centuries to come.

13

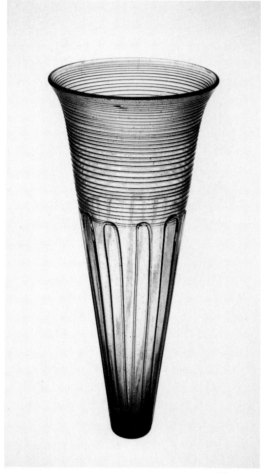

14

14.
This delightful functional cone beaker, free-blown in light amber glass with applied loops and threading, exhibits much more glassmaking skill than do many *Waldglas* drinking vessels of this period. Rhineland, Belgium or northern France, early sixth century. Height: 23.5 cm. (9¼ in.). Corning Museum of Glass, Corning, N.Y.

15.
Claw beaker of green glass free-blown and ornamented with applied threading and "claws." This rare medieval drinking vessel was found in a grave in Castle Eden, Durham, England. Rhineland or England, late fifth or early sixth century. Height: 19 cm. (7½ in.). British Museum, London

15

The Islamic World The vaselike mosque lamps with elaborate enameled and gilded designs fired on the glass surface are probably the best-known examples of Islamic glass decoration from the thirteenth and fourteenth centuries. Produced primarily in Damascus and Aleppo, these lamps, with their arabesque scrollwork, blazons and highly complimentary inscriptions to sultans and lesser palace dignitaries, provide tantalizing glimpses into the mysterious Islamic world. Although called lamps, the free-blown urn-shaped objects were actually shades designed to hold the oil lamps that illuminated the mosques. Usually they had three or six applied glass handles to hold the chains which suspended them from the ceiling. The colors of the opaque enamels in which the designs were painted included blue, green and white, with red used often for backgrounds and almost always for outlining the principal decorative elements. Gilded borders and design motifs gave an added richness to the overall effect (colorplate 6). Even finer enameled work, with as many as eight colors, was done on vases, pilgrim flasks and flaring beakers probably made as presentation pieces.

Glass cutting was one of the most highly developed decorating techniques of Islamic glassmakers and brought world recognition and leadership to the Islamic glassmaking centers from about the eighth to the twelfth century. As early as the fourth and fifth centuries Sassanian glass cutters were producing hemispherical bowls and other useful objects with overall cut decorations in honeycomb patterns (plate 16), concave circles and other geometric designs. By the ninth century the craft was flourishing, and during the next three hundred

16.
Sassanian bowl of thick green glass with cut decoration in a honeycomb pattern foreshadowing designs used centuries later by English and Irish glass cutters. The surface, which was polished at the time the bowl was produced, is now weathered and flaking. Northern Iran, fifth–sixth century. Diameter: 11.5 cm. (4½ in.). Smithsonian Institution, National Museum of History and Technology

17

17.
The relief-cut stylized birds, foliage and scrolls decorating this pinkish glass Hedwig beaker are reminiscent of earlier Islamic rock-crystal masterpieces. Possibly made in Egypt, twelfth century. Height: 8.6 cm. (3⅜ in.). Corning Museum of Glass, Corning, N.Y.

18.
The facility with which twelfth-century Persian glassworkers were able to execute tooled decoration "at the fire" is dramatically demonstrated by the ornamentation of this free-blown glass bottle. Originally made of clear glass, it is now iridescent due to burial. The pincered trailing and elaborate handles show the influence of Islamic tenth-century rock-crystal stylings. Iran, c. twelfth century. Height: 26.7 cm. (10½ in.). Corning Museum of Glass, Corning, N.Y.

18

19.
Persian and Venetian traits are apparent in the free-blown blue glass ewer (left) and elegant brown glass sprinkler with its swirled neck (center). The dark brown glass ewer (right) is mold-blown with applied handle and spout. Iran, seventeenth and eighteenth centuries. Height of sprinkler: 31 cm. (12¼ in.). Cooper-Hewitt Museum, gift of Rodman Wanamaker

years Islamic artisans produced some of the most exquisite relief-cut designs in the history of the industry.

Unfortunately, most of the fine earlier cut-glass examples are now in fragments, but one group of later period beakers having a twelfth-century dating has survived virtually intact. These glasses are known as the Hedwig beakers because two examples of this type were thought to have belonged to Saint Hedwig. Although the glasses have been attributed to craftsmen in Egypt, some authorities feel they may have been made elsewhere. Whatever their origin, these handsome twelfth-century beakers represent a superb mastery of the glass cutter's art (plate 17). Islamic glassmakers also produced hand-blown glass, using many of the techniques developed by their Roman predecessors. These useful and ornamental wares were often decorated "at the fire," and some of the elegant long-necked bottles seem to anticipate later Venetian extravagances (plate 18).

The Persian glass industry ceased to be productive at the end of the fourteenth century as a result of the Mongol conquests. After Tamerlane subdued the Syrians in 1400 and carried off their glassmakers to Samarkand, the industry in that area virtually ceased. Almost no important glassmaking was carried on in Islamic areas until the Venetians revived the craft in Iran in the seventeenth century. These seventeenth- and eighteenth-century productions often reflect a delightful mingling of Venetian and Persian influences (plate 19). They again drew attention to Islamic glassmaking and recaptured some of the prestige lost in the fifteenth century to the Venetian glass industry already well-established at Murano.

Colorplate 6.
The swirled, enameled and superbly cut decorations of these glass pieces show the diverse skills of Islamic glassworkers over five centuries. Left to right: flask, eleventh–twelfth century; mosque lamp, Syria, c. 1350; cup, probably Iran, ninth century. Height of lamp: 30.5 cm. (12 in.). Corning Museum of Glass, Corning, N.Y.

3 Venice and Its Influence

The Venetian industry is one of the most glamorous in the history of glass. Situated on the island of Murano, across the lagoon from Venice, it has produced some of the most fascinating artistic and technical achievements of the glassmaking art (colorplate 7).

Glass was made in the area of Venice in Roman times, but the craft died out with the fall of the Empire. The present industry began in the late tenth century, and glass was being exported in the thirteenth. Little is known about these early productions, but they may have been wine bottles, tumblers and window glass. In 1291 the glassworkers were moved from Venice proper to the nearby island of Murano. The new location not only removed the fire hazard of the furnaces from Venice but it made the workers virtual prisoners in the island enclave. This isolation was intentional because the glass industry had become so important to the Venetian economy that the Doge and affluent merchants were determined to keep the glassworkers from taking their secrets to potential competitors. Any glassworker who left the island was automatically placed under sentence of death "in absentia." To compensate for their loss of freedom, the artisans were given many social privileges, including permission for their daughters to marry into the nobility. Regardless of these concessions and in spite of the penalties, many Venetian glassworkers escaped. By the sixteenth and seventeenth centuries techniques learned from these fugitives were being practiced in many European countries, including Austria, the Netherlands, France, Germany, Bohemia, Spain and Great Britain.

While the runaway Venetians were probably the greatest contributors to the rejuvenation of glassmaking throughout Europe, a rival Italian glassmaking center at Altare, near Genoa, was also responsible for setting up a number of European glass centers. The Altarist establishment was started about the fourteenth century, probably by glassmakers from Lorraine, France. By the mid-fifteenth century

Colorplate 7.
By the sixteenth century the Maestri di Murano were expert in most of the complicated glassmaking techniques in use today. These dragon-stem goblets, *cristallo* and milk white glass bowls with enameled decorations, filigree compote and so-called lace-glass drinking vessel with its metal "whistle handle" are a few of their achievements. Venice, sixteenth and seventeenth century. Height of goblet on left: 26.2 cm. (10¼ in.). Corning Museum of Glass, Corning, N.Y.

Altarist productions were so similar to many of the Venetian styles that it is now impossible to tell whether undocumented pieces in these traditional forms were made in Venice, Altare or the other glass-making centers where these artisans worked. In contrast to the restrictions placed on the movements of Venetian craftsmen, Altarists were encouraged by their guild to carry their glassmaking knowledge to other locations. One of the best known of their "missionary" efforts was the important glassmaking center in Nevers, France (see page 53), which they established in the sixteenth century.

The Altarists were never a serious threat, however, and during the fourteenth and fifteenth centuries the Venetian glass industry achieved the supremacy it was to maintain for more than two hundred years. Contributing to the Venetians' leadership was their rediscovery of manganese as a decolorizer for soda-lime glass. Although the Romans had known about this element, its use in glassmaking had been lost for centuries in western Europe. The glass the Venetians made with their improved formula was called *cristallo* because it resembled rock crystal (quartz). Although a clear colorless glass was their objective, for many years *cristallo* often had pale yellow, smoky brown or even blackish tinges, which nevertheless provided pleasing backgrounds for painted enamel decorations (colorplate 1, see page 6). By the mid-sixteenth century these defects were overcome, and *cristallo* became the clear colorless glass so long desired.

Equally important in establishing the supremacy of Venetian glass were the mid-fifteenth-century free-blown goblets, standing cups and other presentation pieces in rich blues, emerald greens, glowing purples and a rare opaque turquoise. These magnificent objects, sometimes painted in opaque enamel colors with processions and portrait medallions, are the earliest glass pieces which can be positively identified as Venetian.

A Venetian specialty, *lattimo* (opaque white or milk white) glass (plate 20), was first made in Murano in the fifteenth century. It was used in the sixteenth century and later, either alone or twisted in spirals with colored threads and encased in clear colorless glass, to make the intricate *latticino* or *filigrana* (filigree) pieces which are still popular Venetian productions (plate 21). In a difficult variation of this process sometimes called *vetro di trina* (lace glass), but more correctly termed *vetro a reticello* (network glass), the white glass threads were criss-crossed in an allover pattern of fine diamonds, each enclosing a small bubble (see colorplate 7). In the eighteenth century this opaque white glass was used to make wares imitating porcelain (colorplate 8).

The type of glass called *millefiori* (thousand flowers) was first made by the Venetians in the late fifteenth century, when they revived the ancient technique used for fused mosaic glass. *Millefiori* is still being made in Italy and elsewhere. In the Venetian technique, glass rods of various colors were arranged in a bundle in any desired pattern.

Colorplate 8.
European ceramists were centuries behind the Chinese in perfecting the formula for hard-paste porcelain. Many eighteenth-century Continental glassmaking centers produced opaque white glass in porcelain styles with painted enamel decorations, like this sprinkler and plate from Venice. The plate, painted with a scene of the Grand Canal, was one of a set brought back to London in 1741 by Horace Walpole. Diameter of plate: 22.4 cm. (8¾ in.). Corning Museum of Glass, Corning, N.Y.

20.
A whimsical miniature shoe, free-blown in amethyst glass with *lattimo* (milk white or opaque white) stripes and traces of gilding. Venice, sixteenth century. Length: 12.8 cm. (5 in.). Collection Jerome Strauss, State College, Penna.

21.
Free-blown *cristallo* covered jar with *latticino* (filigree) and *lattimo* stripes in opaque white glass. Venice, late sixteenth–early seventeenth century. Height with cover: 33 cm. (13 in.). Corning Museum of Glass, Corning, N.Y.

22.
Miniature ewer made in a variation of the fused mosaic glass technique called *millefiori* (thousand flowers) by the Venetians. Colored rod sections embedded in clear glass; silver gilt mounts. Venice, sixteenth century. Height: 12.6 cm. (4⅞ in.). British Museum, London

23.
Calcedonio-glass flask blown in marbleized glass imitating the semiprecious stone chalcedony, as the name suggests. Venice, c. 1500. Height: 37.5 cm. (14¾ in.). Victoria and Albert Museum, London

24.
Ice-glass beaker. Ice glass (sometimes also called crackle glass) was first produced by sixteenth-century Venetian glassmakers. Venice, 1550–1600. Height: 20.4 cm. (8 in.). Victoria and Albert Museum, London, Buckley Loan

This pattern can be seen when viewed from the end of the bundle. The bundle of rods is then heated until fused and, while molten, pulled out into a rod which will contain the original pattern in miniature regardless of how far the rod is extended. After cooling, sections of this rod are cut into segments about a quarter of an inch thick. These are placed in a mold side by side in a mosaic pattern. They are then heated in the mold until fused, when they can be removed and shaped further as desired (plate 22). Many other uses have been made of these cane or rod sections. The *millefiori* paperweights made in France in the mid-nineteenth century are well-known examples of this technique (see page 57).

In the sixteenth century the Venetian glassblowers produced *ice glass*. To make this, the parison is plunged into water to crackle the hot glass surface, but reheated before the glass cracks all the way through. This fuses the crackled portion back together, leaving the scars of the crackling in an allover pattern suggesting cracked ice (plate 24). The effect can also be obtained by rolling the parison in crushed glass which has been placed on the marver and reheating the fragments enough to fuse them to the outside of the piece.

Window glass and mirrors were an important part of Venetian glass production at least as early as the sixteenth century. In the seventeenth century Venetian exports of mirrors to France posed such a problem to the French economy that French officials tried to induce Italian glassmakers to set up mirror factories in France. Even after French plate-glass production ended the Venetian monopoly in the early eighteenth century, Murano continued to export mirrors with ornate glass frames all over the world. In addition to mirrors and frames, elaborate chandeliers, candelabra, sconces, table centerpieces and accessories fabricated in crystal and colored glasses have continued to be staples of Venetian production.

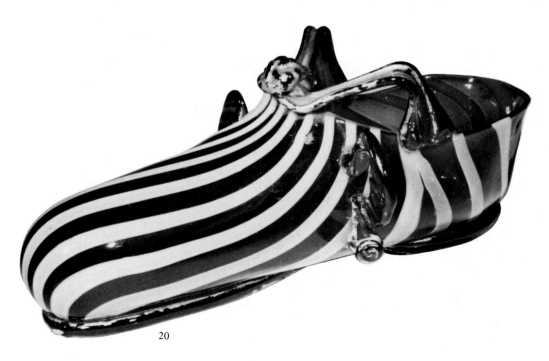

20

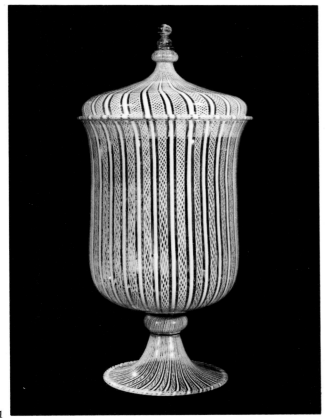

21

22

23   24

Like their ancient predecessors, Venetian artisans were intrigued by the similarity of glass to gems and semiprecious stones. The names of various handsome types of glass—aventurine, onyx, agate and *calcedonio* (plate 23)—suggest a few of the expensive substances the Venetians imitated. The Maestri di Murano devised so many innovations and technical triumphs over the centuries that it is impossible to mention and describe all their glassmaking achievements. It is safe to say, however, that no artisans since the Romans have made a greater contribution to glassmaking.

Germany, Bohemia, Silesia and Austria   The fugitive Venetian and emigrant Altarist glassmakers were largely responsible for the rejuvenation of the glass industry in central and western Europe, which began about the sixteenth century. Their influence produced the handsome *façon de Venise* (plate 25) and *façon d'Altare* styles found in the productions of nearly every important European glassmaking center during the sixteenth and seventeenth centuries. Delicate freeblown compotes and striking covered jars, often with mold-blown stems in the shape of human face masks, appeared. Many pieces are so similar to their Italian prototypes that they defy positive attribution. As the new styles became established, the novel techniques required to produce them stimulated local glassmakers to develop their own regional forms, which sometimes incorporated Venetian features.

The German drinking vessels of the sixteenth and seventeenth centuries clearly demonstrate this interesting phenomenon (colorplate 9). Communal drinking was a way of life, and the functional forms and amazing sizes of these glasses as well as their wonderful German names intrigue layman and connoisseur alike. The stately and cylindrical *Stangenglas* (pole glass) was covered on the outside with pointed prunts which enhanced its rugged beauty and assured a firm grip (plate 26), while the graceful *Römer* (wineglass) had a globular bowl and prunted stem combining beauty with utility. Actually both the *Stangenglas* and the *Römer* were developments of the *Krautstrunk* (cabbage stem), a small beaker with either straight or slightly bowed sides covered with pointed prunts, which originated in the fifteenth century. Strangely enough this earlier drinking vessel was sometimes used as a reliquary. Several have been found with relics of saints sealed inside.

The *Passglas* must have been one of the most popular party glasses of its day. This tall, sometimes tapered cylinder, usually on a high-blown foot showing Venetian influence, had applied glass or enameled horizontal rings spaced at equal intervals from top to bottom. These rings indicated where each guest should start and stop his draught. Many exciting incidents developed when imbibers failed to heed the limits set by these functional rings (plate 27).

Colorplate 9.
Some of the exotic functional forms of German sixteenth- and seventeenth-century drinking vessels are (left to right) pattern-molded beaker; *Kuttrolf* (gurgling bottle) with *latticino* stripes on globular body; *Humpen* (tall beaker) with enamel-painted decoration depicting the annual parade of the *Halloren* (salt panners), Saxony, dated 1679; *Römer* (wineglass), seventeenth century; *Maigelein* (cup), late fifteenth–early sixteenth century; *Daumenglas* (drinking barrel or thumb glass), seventeenth century; *Krautstrunk* (cabbage stem), sixteenth century. Height of *Humpen*: 27.7 cm. (10⅞ in.). Corning Museum of Glass, Corning, N.Y.

25.
Façon de Venise covered goblet free-blown in clear slightly grayish glass with applied decorations and mold-blown mask stem. Scrolled medallions, border and other decorations in diamond-point engraving. Austria, Innsbruck, c. 1580. Height: 31.9 cm. (12½ in.). Corning Museum of Glass, Corning, N.Y.

26.
Stangenglas (pole glass), a handsome German communal drinking vessel, free-blown in bluish green glass and decorated with vertical rows of pointed prunts. Probably Rhineland, early sixteenth century. Height: 26 cm. (10¼ in.). British Museum, London

One of the largest and most popular of these communal glasses was the *Humpen*, an uncomplicated cylindrical vessel having an applied base ring and sometimes a cover. In the seventeenth and eighteenth centuries these beer glasses were often twelve to fifteen inches tall and held two to three quarts. By the nineteenth and twentieth centuries some covered *Humpen* were as tall as two feet. Their large plain surfaces were ideally suited to decorations; many were almost completely engulfed with enameled and/or engraved depictions, including hunting scenes, processions, commemorative subjects and elaborate inscriptions. The earliest-known dated enameled *Humpen*, now in the British Museum, has the date 1571 in its decoration and was painted in Bohemia. Probably the most celebrated were the *Reichsadlerhumpen*, which, as the name suggests, were ornamented with decorations depicting the imperial double-headed eagle (*Reichsadler*) bearing on its spreading wings the coats of arms of the electors and other officials of the Holy Roman Empire (plate 28).

A lighter note was introduced by the *Scherzglas* (joke glass), also called a siphon or "trick" glass, in which a hollow blown-glass animal figure was attached to a glass tube. This was placed over a vertical rod projecting upward from the inside of a goblet. Holes in the animal's

25

26

27

27.
Passglas, a German communal drinking vessel with five applied rings spaced to designate the portion each guest should drink before passing it on. Painted in grisaille between the rings is a triumphal procession. The inscription, in translation, reads, "The solemn rejoicing of the electorate of Bavaria on the occasion of the baptismal ceremonies of the most illustrious prince and lord, the Lord Maximilian Emanuel Louis Mary Joseph, in the year 1662." Germany, third quarter of the seventeenth century. Height: 22.6 cm. (8⅞ in.). British Museum, London

28.
Reichsadlerhumpen, a communal drinking glass, so called because the painted enamel decorations depict the *Reichsadler*, the double-headed eagle of the Holy Roman Empire, bearing shields of the electors on its wings. Bohemia, dated 1574. Height: 26.4 cm. (10⅜ in.). Corning Museum of Glass, Corning, N.Y.

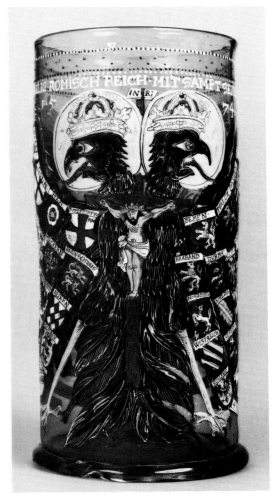

mouth and elsewhere were used like a straw to suck the liquid from the glass. The "trick" was to cover all but one of the holes with a finger or fingers while drinking or no liquid would rise in the tube (plate 29). Other humorous glass shapes were bottlelike forms of animals (plate 30), shoes, pistols and horns.

Schwarzlot was a sophisticated enamel decoration painted in black monochrome with occasional red and gold accents. This style was introduced about 1660 in Nuremberg by Johann Schaper (plate 31), who also painted on stained glass and porcelain. Schaper was one of the independent painters called *Hausmaler* because they painted at home or in their own workshops rather than at the factory where the glass or porcelain was made. A number of them signed their work. Thus the names of Schaper, Daniel and Ignaz Preissler, who worked in Bohemia and Silesia, and Abraham Helmhack, who painted in Nuremberg in the eighteenth century, are familiar to collectors today.

A rare decoration, known in antiquity, was revived about 1730 in Bohemia, where it was called *Zwischengoldglas* (gold between glass). In this process a design in gold and/or silver leaf was placed on the outer surface of a beaker. The beaker was then slid inside another of the same shape but enough larger to enclose it like a snug sleeve. The two glasses were then cemented together at the top and often sealed at the bottom with a glass disk, thus enclosing the gold-leaf design between them (plate 32). A few goblets and other pieces with *Zwischengoldglas* medallions are known. Although the process was continued at intervals in Bohemia and Germany into the nineteenth century, the best eighteenth-century examples were made at one or two Bohemian workshops between 1730 and 1755.

One of the most important contributions of late sixteenth- and seventeenth- and eighteenth-century Bohemian, German and Silesian glass artisans was the revival and perfection of wheel-engraving on glass. As early as 1500 B.C., Egyptian artists had used various forms of abrasion to decorate glass. From that time on there were intermittent periods when lapidaries did intaglio engravings on glass, usually in the same styles they were using on gems and semiprecious stones.

In western Europe lapidary techniques were little used on glass after the fifth century A.D. From about the fourteenth to the sixteenth century fine chalices, footed bowls and other luxury objects were being produced by Italian and Bohemian lapidaries in costly materials including onyx, chalcedony, agate and rock crystal. One of these artisans, Caspar Lehmann, chief lapidary at the court of Emperor Rudolf II in Prague, was long credited with reviving and adapting these techniques to glass in the early seventeenth century, for a wheel-engraved beaker of his, signed *C. Leman* [sic] *F. 1605*, is the earliest-known dated example from this period. Recently, however, research in Germany uncovered several fine wheel-engraved panels made in Munich at least as early as the 1580s.

29

30

31

29.
Siphon, or "trick," glass. The hollow double-headed animal form is attached to a glass tube, which when properly held allows the drinker to siphon or suck the liquid from the glass. Germany, early eighteenth century. Height: 28 cm. (11 in.). Corning Museum of Glass, Corning, N.Y.

30.
Dog-shaped bottle free-blown in greenish glass with a pewter stopper set in the tail. Germany, sixteenth century. Length: 24.5 cm. (9⅝ in.). Smithsonian Institution, National Museum of History and Technology, R. Strasser Collection

31.
Covered beaker painted in *Schwarzlot*, a type of black monochrome, with portraits of Emperor Leopold I and Empress Margaret, by Johann Schaper, who introduced the style. Germany, third quarter of the seventeenth century. Height: 9 cm. (3½ in.). Corning Museum of Glass, Corning, N.Y.

A type of covered goblet called a *Pokal*, first made in Nuremberg about 1660, lent itself beautifully to wheel-engraved decoration. Usually a presentation piece engraved with a coat of arms or other appropriate insignia, it was the most prestigious German communal drinking vessel used at upper-class and court functions (plate 33).

Two types of wheel-engraving practiced in the seventeenth and eighteenth centuries were called by the German names *Tiefschnitt* (intaglio) and the more difficult *Hochschnitt* (relief). Clear colorless glass was usually preferred for this work, as both types of engraving showed to better advantage in that medium (plates 34, 35 and 36).

A wide variety of tablewares had fine *Tiefschnitt* engravings, including the "sweetmeat" glasses (plate 37) which are now the delight of collectors. Another type which can only be considered by wealthy collectors are the superbly engraved glasses by Gottfried Spiller (plate 38), a Potsdam artist who worked in the late seventeenth and early eighteenth centuries. There were also some engravings, now very rare, on the gold ruby glass which had been perfected about 1679 by Johann Kunckel, manager of an important Potsdam glasshouse. Kunckel was also associated with the development of the so-called chalk glass, about 1680, in which the lime content was increased by the addition of chalk. This provided a better clear colorless glass than had been previously available on the Continent, but it was still less brilliant and resonant than the English lead crystal perfected by Ravenscroft about 1676 (see page 73).

In the last quarter of the eighteenth century the baroque and rococo styles of engraving were declining in popularity and the established English and Irish cut and engraved patterns were coming into favor on the Continent. A new interest was growing in colored glass, and for several decades beginning about the 1820s the Biedermeier period taste dominated Bohemian glass production (colorplate 10). New colors were developed and decorated with cutting, engraving, enameling and gilding. Cased glass in two or more layers with designs cut through the outer casings (colorplate 11) was made in quantity and influenced style trends as far away as America.

A cheaper process, which gave somewhat the same effect as cased glass, involved spraying or painting the glass blanks or even the finished cut pieces with red or yellow stain. This stain was then fired in a muffle kiln to give it permanence and engraved or cut in designs similar to the cased-glass pieces (colorplate 12).

In the first decades of the nineteenth century the increase in travel by the more affluent middle classes created a greater market for souvenirs of all kinds. The glassmakers responded with an ample supply of ornamental pieces, which varied from hastily contrived trifles to well-executed articles which are now valued treasures.

Among the artists who produced some of these finer objects was Samuel Mohn, who had developed transparent enamels for painting

32.
Tumbler with *Zwischengoldglas* (gold between glass) decoration. Bohemia, c. 1730–40. Height: 6.8 cm. (2⅝ in.). Royal Ontario Museum, Toronto

Colorplate 10.
Mid-nineteenth-century Bohemian glass-makers often introduced ingenious decorative effects such as the optical motif in this monumental covered jar. An additional feature is the ruby glass casing with its cut and engraved decorations. Height overall: 53.5 cm. (21⅛ in.). Cooper-Hewitt Museum, gift of James B. Ford

Colorplate 11.
The technical proficiency of the mid-nineteenth-century Bohemian glassworkers is demonstrated in the double casings (two outer layers of glass) on the *Pokal* (left) and beaker. The engraving on the center *Pokal* depicts Cologne Cathedral and may have been made in Germany. The beaker has a sulphide portrait medallion bust marked *E. Kirchner*. Height of beaker: 12.1 cm. (4¾ in.). Corning Museum of Glass, Corning, N.Y.

Colorplate 12.
Biedermeier taste is reflected in these
Bohemian drinking glasses. Cut paneled
beaker with oval bosses and gilding, c.
1825–40. Massive goblet also panel-cut
with stained portions and the coats of
arms of Austria, Russia and Prussia
painted in enamel colors, c. 1835–40.
Mineral-water glass with four views of
Teplitz cut and engraved through the
ruby stain, c. 1856. Height of glass with
cover: 21 cm. (8¼ in.). Corning Museum
of Glass, Corning, N.Y.

33.
Covered goblets called *Pokale* were the most elegant seventeenth- and eighteenth-century communal drinking vessels. All three shown here have wheel-engraved decorations. The *Pokal* at left, made in Potsdam about 1730–50, also has gilded accents. The center *Pokal*, with its dark green glass foot and cased bowl, is typical of a long-stemmed design that originated in Nuremberg, 1660–80. The double *Pokal* was another exotic seventeenth-century creation of German drinking-glass designers. Overall height of double *Pokal*: 40 cm. (15¾ in.). Corning Museum of Glass, Corning, N.Y.

34.
Plaque of clear colorless glass with one of the earliest-known examples of *Tiefschnitt* (intaglio) wheel-engraving. The scene shows Tomyris, Queen of Massagetae, dropping the head of Cyrus, King of Persia, into a skin of blood. Engraved by Hans Wessler, Nuremberg, Germany, 1610–20. Height: 15.5 cm. (6⅛ in.). Corning Museum of Glass, Corning, N.Y.

34

33

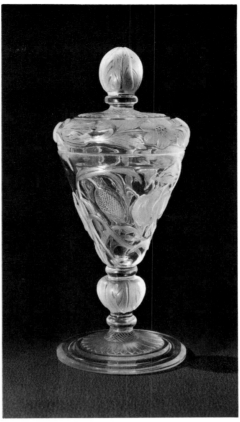

35.
Free-blown goblet with fine intaglio wheel- and diamond-engraved figures symbolizing the Four Continents. Facet-cut stem. Germany, probably Hesse or Lauenstein, eighteenth century. Height: 25.7 cm. (10⅛ in.). Cooper-Hewitt Museum, gift of the Trustees of the Estate of James Hazen Hyde

36.
Free-blown *Pokal* and cover of clear colorless glass with superb *Hochschnitt* (relief) decoration of baroque flowers and leaves. Germany, Brandenburg, late seventeenth century. Height: 28.6 cm. (11¼ in.). Collection Jerome Strauss, State College, Penna.

37.
"Sweetmeat" glass, fashionable in the late seventeenth and eighteenth centuries for serving nuts, candies and dried fruits toward the end of a meal. Delicate wheel-engravings enhance the bowl and foot. Faceted stem. Silesia, c. 1730. Height: 11.8 cm. (4⅝ in.). Smithsonian Institution, National Museum of History and Technology

38.
Elaborately engraved covered beaker with designs in both *Tiefschnitt* and *Hochschnitt* techniques, including the monogram of Elector Frederick III of Brandenburg. Possibly the work of Gottfried Spiller, one of the best late seventeenth- and early eighteenth-century glass engravers. Germany, Potsdam, c. 1700. Height: 22 cm. (8⅝ in.). Corning Museum of Glass, Corning, N.Y.

35

36

37

38

39.
Portrait plaque in fine intaglio engraving. Signed by Dominik Bimann, the best engraver of his era (1826–57). Bohemia, Prague, dated 1834. Diameter: 9.5 cm. (3¾ in.). Corning Museum of Glass, Corning, N.Y.

Colorplate 13.
Semiprecious stones and Chinese lacquer inspired these very rare early nineteenth-century Bohemian glass creations. The vase and covered box are Lithyalin glass made by Friedrich Egermann c. 1828–40. Height of vase: 30.5 cm. (12 in.). The plate is Hyalith glass made c. 1820–30. Diameter of plate: 20.5 cm. (8 in.). Corning Museum of Glass, Corning, N.Y.

Colorplate 14.
Clear glass beakers with exquisite miniature enamel decorations painted by two of the most famous early nineteenth-century artists. The view of Meissen is signed by Samuel Mohn, Dresden, Germany; the portrait of Alexander I, Czar of Russia, painted c. 1815–25, is signed with the initials *AK*, which stand for Anton Kothgasser. Height of beaker with view of Meissen: 10.2 cm. (4 in.). Corning Museum of Glass, Corning, N.Y.

on glass. Mohn and his son worked first in Dresden, then in Vienna from about 1811. Another famous artist, Anton Kothgasser, who had been a painter at the Imperial Porcelain Factory in Vienna, was particularly skillful in painting local scenes with almost photographic accuracy. His portrait miniatures painted on glass beakers show great sensitivity and complete control of the medium. Pieces signed by Mohn or Kothgasser are now mostly in museums or private collections (colorplate 14). Unsigned nineteenth-century pieces which have been attributed to these artists are more likely to have been the work of their pupils or imitators.

Much fine copper wheel-engraving was also done throughout the nineteenth century. One of the most skillful engravers of that or any other century was Dominik Bimann, who worked from the 1820s to the 1850s in Bohemia and specialized in miniature intaglio portraits (plate 39).

The increasing popularity of colored glass in the early nineteenth century encouraged glassmakers to experiment with new effects. Many new colors were developed, including opalescent and other unusual shadings of the already fashionable blues, greens, yellows, amethysts and rubies. As in every age, glass made in imitation of, or inspired by, more precious substances tempted the skills of glass technicians. One of these imitations was Hyalith, an opaque black or dark red glass that resembled Chinese lacquer. It was made from 1820 to 1830 at a factory in southern Bohemia owned by Franz August, Count von Buquoy (colorplate 13).

Another technical as well as artistic achievement in nineteenth-century glass was Lithyalin, a nearly opaque marbled glass made in several color combinations. The laminated structure of this glass was brought out by cutting and polishing the surface in flat vertical panels. This glass was patented about 1828 by the noted Bohemian glassmaker Friedrich Egermann, whose factory was located in Blottendorf near the famous glassmaking center of Haida, Bohemia (see colorplate 13).

Glassmaking centers have continued in these central European areas to the present, and their productions are popular collector's items. J. & L. Lobmeyr, founded in Vienna in 1823, has produced some of the world's finest decorative glass articles and tablewares (plate 40), including superb wheel-engraved and cut pieces. Their elegant chandeliers are found in opera houses and palaces on both sides of the Atlantic. In nearby Czechoslovakia the Moser factory in Karlovy Vary has a distinguished history and has produced fine luxury and useful wares since 1857. Another Bohemian factory, founded in Klostermühle in 1836, was acquired by Johann Lötz in 1840. After Lötz died in 1848, his widow continued the factory under the name Johann Lötz Witwe. In the 1890s it was particularly noted for its iridescent Art Nouveau glass, often distinctive in style and still available to collectors.

COLORPLATE 13

COLORPLATE 14

40.
Extremely delicate blown-glass table-wares designed for J. & L. Lobmeyr include wineglasses and lidded candy dishes by Oswald Haerdtl and a vase with lid by Hans H. Rath. Height of vase: 36 cm. (14⅛ in.). Austria, Vienna, twentieth century. Cooper-Hewitt Museum, purchase in memory of Georgiana L. McClellan (glasses and candy dishes) and gift of J. & L. Lobmeyr (vase)

41.
Wineglasses free-blown in lead-crystal glass. At left, wheel-engraved decoration of billing doves in rococo scroll signed by Jacob Sang and dated 1758. At center, diamond-point-engraved inscription, *Studia et Artes*, signed by Lokhorst Scrip and dated 1765. At right, wheel-engraved decoration of clasped hands in a baroque panel signed by Jacob Sang and dated 1761. Height of wineglass on right: 17.6 cm. (6⅞ in.). Dutch decorations on English glass. Victoria and Albert Museum, London, Buckley Loans

Holland and Belgium   Glassmaking fashions and techniques in central Europe and the Low Countries were so intertwined during and after the sixteenth century that it is impossible to draw sharp distinctions between them. While national and regional styles emerged at intervals, they were soon copied or adapted by any glassmaker who had the capabilities and a demand for these productions.

During the sixteenth and seventeenth centuries Dutch and Belgian glassmakers produced fine quality free-blown glass. Some faithfully followed Venetian and German traditions while others showed a delightful mingling of contemporary styles. Wheel-engravings during most of the seventeenth and eighteenth centuries were dominated by German and Bohemian styles even when the blanks used were English lead crystal. Several fine engravers signed their work. One of the most famous was Jacob Sang, probably a Thuringian, who worked in Amsterdam in the 1750s and 1760s (plate 41). His specialties were allegorical figures, coats of arms and ships, which he often did as special orders with lengthy inscriptions guaranteed to please the wealthy shipowners.

While Dutch and Belgian glassworkers clearly demonstrated their ability to compete favorably with contemporary free-blown *façon de Venise* and wheel-engraved wares of England and Germany, their seventeenth-century diamond-point and their eighteenth-century diamond-stipple engraved pieces were by far their greatest achievements.

Diamond-point engraving consists of scratching designs on the glass surface with a stylus having a diamond point or some other material hard enough to scratch the glass. The Venetians and Austrians (see plate 25) used this technique in the sixteenth century, and their styles were continued in the Netherlands throughout the seventeenth century. In the first part of that century many of these engravings were done by gifted amateurs, who usually signed their work. One of the finest pieces, which is unsigned, is a beaker engraved with figures of the Pope and Christ and with satirical Dutch verses. Dated 1604, it is now in the Rijksmuseum, Amsterdam.

A variation of the diamond-point engraving technique—*diamond-stipple engraving*—was introduced in Holland by Frans Greenwood, who was born in Rotterdam in 1680 and worked in Dordrecht from 1722 until his death in 1761. In this process the design is stippled on the glass surface by tapping dots on the glass with a diamond-pointed stylus. Shading is achieved by the spacing of the dots. The closer the dots, the whiter that part of the design appears. In the finest pieces the shading is so delicately controlled that the design almost seems to have been breathed on the glass. Although some stippling had been done together with the scratched lines in the earlier diamond-point engravings, Greenwood is credited with being the first to use the diamond-stipple technique for the entire design (plate 42).

An equally well known name in Dutch diamond-stipple engraving is David Wolff (1732–1798), who worked in The Hague during most of his career. His later designs were even more delicate than Greenwood's, and his signed pieces rank with the best diamond-point and diamond-stipple engravings on glass. Lesser-known diamond-point engravers who signed their work include Aert Schouman (1710–1798) and Jacobus van den Blijk (1736–1814). Fine work by anonymous artisans is also in the collections of the leading European and American museums. Whether signed or anonymous these Dutch diamond-point and diamond-stipple engravings are masterpieces of glass decoration and were unrivaled until about the mid-twentieth century, when the art was revived in England by Laurence Whistler (b. 1912), whose superb diamond-stipple engravings on goblets, bowls and windowpanes have justly received worldwide acclaim.

Two glass factories of this region which have set high standards from their founding to the present are N. V. Vereenigde Glasfabriek, Leerdam, Holland (begun in 1765), and the Cristalleries du Val-Saint-Lambert in Belgium (begun in 1826). Val-Saint-Lambert's Art Nouveau and cameo glass made at the turn of the century and Leerdam's Unicas (one of a kind) produced in the twentieth century are only a few of their objects which are prized by collectors.

42.
Free-blown goblet of English lead glass. Portrait of a man in diamond-stipple engraving is by Frans Greenwood, the first artist to use this technique. The Netherlands, Dordrecht, dated 1746. Height: 25.5 cm. (10 in.). Corning Museum of Glass, Corning, N.Y.

France The magnificent stained-glass windows of Chartres, Notre Dame and Sainte Chapelle contain some of the richest colors ever developed in glass. Throughout the centuries they have inspired worshipers, enhanced the architecture of the buildings in which they are placed and challenged later stained-glass artists to emulate their beauty. These vibrant masterpieces are undoubtedly the greatest contribution of French medieval and early Renaissance stained-glass artists to the development of artistic glass, but other beautiful stained glass was made as well (colorplate 15). Most of the glass for these creations was made on the site or produced in the window-glass factories of Normandy, Lorraine and Burgundy. These French glasshouses made flat glass for local cathedrals and exported it to other countries, including England, where very little fine colored glass was being made at that time. They also supplied itinerant glaziers, who carried stocks of glass along with their tools and made installations as far away as Spain and Sweden, where some twelfth- and thirteenth-century churches have windows of French glass.

With so much activity in stained-glass production, it is surprising that relatively little luxury glass or fine French tablewares have survived from the sixteenth and seventeenth centuries. The finer French glasswares which have survived are often in *façon de Venise* styles and could have been made by resident Venetian and Altarist glassmakers after they came to France. Some of these goblets, tazzas and wineglasses have rather dubious French attributions based mostly on their enameled decorations showing French coats of arms and inscriptions. Useful wares were often continuations of the earlier *verre de fougère* (bracken glass) made in the forest glasshouses in greenish or yellowish glass of mediocre quality.

One of the important early French glassmaking centers was Nevers, founded in the sixteenth century by artisans from Altare, Italy, who had been brought to France by the Duke of Nevers. The duke's welcome, perpetuated by later officials, attracted both Venetian and Altarist glassworkers in such numbers that by the eighteenth century Nevers was known as "Little Murano." While a great deal of Altarist- and Venetian-style glassware must have been made in Nevers, its best-known productions were small animal and human figures, first made in the late sixteenth century. These were fabricated by a process known as *lampworking*, in which glass rods, tubes or other glass pieces were formed into the desired objects by heating them in the flame of a "lamp" or some laboratory-type burner. These "toys" ranged from figures representing the seasons (plate 43), deities and royalty to Italian Comedy characters and peasants. They were used singly or in groups, often placed in fanciful settings with castles, trees and rocks made of glass, wood or other materials. As with every successful type of glass, Nevers figures were soon copied by workers elsewhere. The figures were made well into the nineteenth century, and lampworking has

Colorplate 15 (overleaf).
A thirteenth-century window from the Abbey of Saint-Germain-des-Prés in Paris shows the typical glass colors of the period. Depicted is a scene from the life of Saint Vincent of Spain showing the saint in chains. France, c. 1245. Width: 55.2 cm. (21¾ in.). Metropolitan Museum of Art, New York, gift of George D. Pratt, 1924

continued as a highly skilled technique used to produce scientific equipment as well as artistic and amusing objects to the present day.

The French plate-glass industry owed its initial success to Bernard Perrot. This talented glassmaker, a native of Altare, Italy, came to France as a young man in 1649 and spent the next sixty years devising new glassmaking processes and colors in the glasshouses of Nevers and Orléans. Among his early accomplishments were patents for a red glass, used for enameling, and an opaque white that resembled porcelain and cameos. He was the first to substitute glass pendants for rock crystal on chandeliers. His greatest technical contribution came in 1688 when he invented a process for casting glass panels (including bas-reliefs). This invention came at a time when the French plate-glass industry was struggling desperately to compete with that of Italy, and the French were importing large quantities of mirrors and plate glass from Venice. Perrot's invention for casting plate glass provided the technical stimulus needed to enable the French plate-glass industry to forge ahead of its Venetian competition and eventually attain world leadership during the eighteenth and nineteenth centuries.

The factory responsible for developing the French plate-glass supremacy was the Manufacture Royale des Glaces de France. It was established in 1695 at Saint-Gobain in the forest region of La Thiérache, where glasshouses had been located for several centuries. Since the eighteenth century Saint-Gobain, as it is now usually called, has been one of the world's largest glassmaking establishments. It has continued its production of flat glass and expanded into many other fields of commercial glassware during the late nineteenth and twentieth centuries.

The production of fine ornamental glass and tablewares developed much more slowly in France than in Bohemia and Germany. But the relatively few eighteenth-century pieces which are known indicate a high degree of glassmaking proficiency and range from fine engraved and enameled wares to imitations of semiprecious stones and porcelain (colorplate 16). The first important eighteenth-century glasshouse, now called the Compagnie des Cristalleries de Baccarat, was established under royal patronage in 1764. The factory operated under difficulties for many years, but by the 1820s its fine crystal-glass tablewares rivaled those being made in England and Ireland. The factory was awarded a gold medal at the Paris National Exhibition in 1823 and in the same year made a table service for Louis XVIII. From then on Baccarat flourished, consistently setting new design trends, developing new colors like opaline or adapting new production methods. An early example of this was their production of pressed lacy glass in competition with American factories in the 1830s.

Another important French factory, the Compagnie des Cristalleries de Saint-Louis, was founded in 1767, just three years after Baccarat and in the same area of Lorraine. Early productions were in German and

43.
Rare figurine representing Summer from a set of the Four Seasons. Made by fusing small rods and other glass pieces together and forming them over the flame of a "lamp," a process called lampworking. France, Nevers, eighteenth century. Height: 22.3 cm. (8¾ in.). Cooper-Hewitt Museum, gift of Frederick P. Victoria

Bohemian styles, and in the 1780s Saint-Louis made some of the first high-quality crystal glass produced in France. During the late eighteenth century the factory experienced the same difficulties as Baccarat, but by the 1820s it too had stabilized its operations and was firmly established as one of Europe's leading glasshouses.

In the 1840s Baccarat, Saint-Louis and a then relatively new factory, Clichy-la-Garenne, near Paris, undertook a novel phase of glass production: paperweights. Originally produced as inexpensive desk ornaments and souvenirs of pleasant visits to France, these jewel-like creations were first made from about 1845 to 1855. Their production was revived, for a time, later in the nineteenth century and again in the twentieth. Other glassmaking centers in Italy, Bohemia, Silesia and England, as well as in America, also made paperweights from the mid-nineteenth century on, often in some of the same styles as their French contemporaries. But the *millefiori* (plate 44), floral, reptile and other specialties of Baccarat, Clichy and Saint-Louis are still considered the finest mid-nineteenth-century productions (colorplate 17). The Clichy factory ceased operations in 1889, but Baccarat and Saint-Louis have continued as two of the foremost European producers of paperweights and other fine glassware to the present day.

Sulphides, sometimes called *crystallo-ceramie*, were another type of decorative element used by the mid-nineteenth-century paperweight makers. These were actually fired clay cameos and other decorative medallions which often had a silvery appearance due to the air trapped in the glass in which they were encased. After some earlier attempts in Bohemia, sulphides were first made and successfully enclosed in glass objects in the late eighteenth and early nineteenth centuries by Barthélemy Desprez, a French artist who had a small porcelain factory in Paris. Their use soon spread to other areas of French production, and by the 1820s they were being made elsewhere in Europe and as far away as America. From about 1820 sulphides were also extremely popular in England, where they were called cameo incrustations and were produced in quantity by the noted English glassmaker Apsley Pellatt.

One of the most significant eras of French artistic glassmaking began in the last quarter of the nineteenth century with the Art Nouveau creations of Émile Gallé (1846–1904). Gallé, a glassmaker's son, worked as a potter, traveled in Germany and studied in London before establishing his glassworks in Nancy, France, in 1874. His early wares, now scarce, were bottles and liquor sets with delicate painted enamel and gilded patterns, but he is most famous for his Art Nouveau cameo-glass vases with their exuberant floral designs etched and engraved through one or more layers of colored glass (plate 45).

Gallé exerted a tremendous influence on his contemporaries and on later glass artists. Many of them emulated his bold flowing signatures, clearly visible on the sides of his vases (see plate 45). After

Colorplate 16.
The two vases with ball-shaped covers are sometimes called wigstands. All these handsome opaque white glass vases, in porcelain styles, have unusually fine decorations painted in polychrome enamels. France, eighteenth century. Height of center vase with cover: 35.3 cm. (13⅞ in.). Corning Museum of Glass, Corning, N.Y.

Colorplate 17.
Nineteenth-century *millefiori* glass was a continuation, with refinements, of fused mosaic processes used by ancient glassmakers. Paperweight on left, a pompom on *latticino* ground, was made by Saint-Louis. The next weight, with its sulphide inclusion of Queen Victoria, the *millefiori* vase and the faceted *millefiori* weight with rose center are by Clichy. The wafer dish with the crown paperweight base was made by Saint-Louis. The *millefiori* tazza with the opaque white twist stem and the triple weight are by Baccarat. France, c. 1845–55. Height of vase: 24.5 cm. (9⅝ in.). Paperweight with Clichy Rose center, collection of the John Nelson Bergstrom Art Center and Museum, Neenah, Wis. All others, Corning Museum of Glass, Corning, N.Y.

44.
Mid-nineteenth-century makers of paperweights used sections of *millefiori* canes enclosed in clear colorless glass to ornament some of their most sought-after productions. Paperweight with Clichy Rose cane in center is by Clichy-la-Garenne. Hand cooler (note distortion of canes due to forming) is by Saint-Louis. Paperweight of close-pack *millefiori* canes, including 1847 date cane, is by Baccarat. France, 1845–55. Average diameter of paperweights: 7.6 cm. (3 in.). Smithsonian Institution, National Museum of History and Technology, Bushee Collection

COLORPLATE 18

COLORPLATE 19

Gallé's death in 1904, his name was still signed on his factory's products, but a star was added to these signatures. The firm continued in business under the direction of Victor Prouvé and others until 1936.

About 1878 Jean Daum, who had come to Nancy from Alsace-Lorraine, took over the struggling Verrerie de Nancy. His older son, Jean-Louis-Auguste, entered the firm in 1879 and in 1887 his younger son, Jean-Antonin, joined. Known as Daum Frères and Cristalleries de Nancy, this successful glass factory is still operated by the Daum family. While their earlier cameo-glass productions were influenced by Gallé's Art Nouveau creations, they later developed many of their own styles and techniques. One of their most successful variations of the cameo-glass technique can be seen in their twentieth-century vases decorated with extremely delicate miniature woodland scenes and landscapes etched and engraved through several layers of glass and accented with enamel painting, which give the illusion of great depth (colorplate 18). The present-day factory continues to produce fine glass in both traditional and advanced styles.

An amazing number of French artists produced and signed their acid-etched cameo glass in Art Nouveau and other styles from about the 1890s to the 1920s. Some of the better known were François-Eugène Rousseau (1827–1891); August-J.-F. Legras (1864–1914); Marcel Goupy (b. 1886); André-Fernand Thesmar (1843–1912); and André Thuret (b. 1898).

Another important glassmaking development of the late nineteenth century in France was the revival of the *pâte de verre* process that had been used by Egyptian and other ancient glassmakers. Among the pioneers in the French revival of this ancient technique (colorplate 19) were two sculptors, Henri Cros (1840–1907) and his son Jean, who achieved considerable success in the late nineteenth and early twentieth centuries. Their *pâte de verre* castings ranged in size from small medallions and bas-relief plaques to statues several feet in height. Other artists whose work in this difficult medium deserves recognition were Albert-Louis Dammouse (1848–1926), another sculptor in Paris, who produced bowls and vases of delicate thinness from about 1898; François-Émile Décorchement (1880–1971), who started making glass in about 1904 and produced noteworthy *pâte de verre* vases and bowls with finely modeled relief designs; Georges Despret (1862–1952), who exhibited his glass in Paris in 1900; Gabriel Argy-Rousseau (b. 1885) and Almeric Walter (1859–1942), both of whom produced fine pieces in the 1920s; and, of course, Gallé and René Lalique, who added the production of *pâte de verre* to their other accomplishments.

Two twentieth-century French artists in glass who made major contributions in widely different glassmaking areas were René Lalique and Maurice Marinot. René-Jules Lalique (1860–1945) is as famous for his magnificent Art Nouveau jewelry, made from about 1885 to 1909, as he is for his glass. From about 1914 until his death,

45.
Cameo glass vase in Art Nouveau style, cased in shades of brown over white. Signed by Gallé. France, c. 1895. Height: 37.5 cm. (14¾ in.). Cooper-Hewitt Museum, gift of Harry Harkness Flagler

Colorplate 18.
Miniature landscapes in cameo glass, often accented with painted enamels, were popular at the turn of the century. This fine example was made by Daum Frères (Cristalleries de Nancy), Nancy, France, late nineteenth–early twentieth century. Height: 25.5 cm. (10 in.). Cooper-Hewitt Museum, purchase in memory of Jacob Schiff

Colorplate 19.
Three important *pâte de verre* pieces. The vase (left) was made by Gabriel Argy-Rousseau. France, c. 1925. Impressed mark above foot: *G. Argy-Rousseau*. Purchase in memory of George A. Hearn. Bowl by François-Émile Décorchement. France, c. 1910. Impressed mark on side: *Decorchemont* in a circle. Purchase in memory of Jacques Séligmann. Oval dish by Henri Cros. France, c. 1900. Unmarked. Length of dish: 23.5 cm. (9¼ in.). Purchase in memory of Georgiana L. McClellan. Cooper-Hewitt Museum

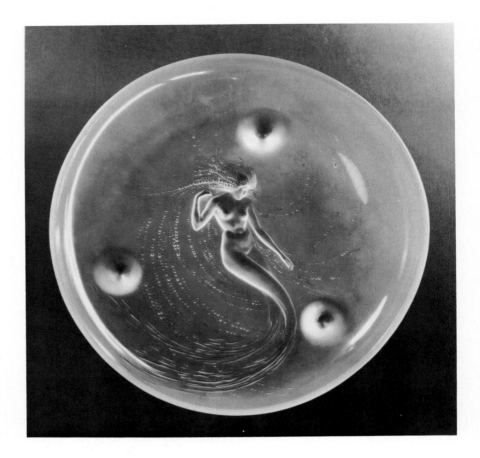

46.
Shallow dish with feet: Sirène. The exterior is satin finish. Impressed mark on side: *R. Lalique.* France, c. 1930. Diameter: 36.9 cm. (14½ in.). Cooper-Hewitt Museum, gift of Jacques Jugeat

47.
Peacock's-head automobile radiator ornament pressed in light blue glass with satin finish and buffed highlights. Impressed mark: *R. Lalique.* Cristallerie Lalique et Cie., France, twentieth century. Height: 22.9 cm. (9 in.). Smithsonian Institution, National Museum of History and Technology

Lalique brought new life to pressed glass. His jeweler's touch is evident in the elegance and detail of the modeling of his molded pieces, which included a few produced by the *cire perdue* (lost wax) process. These were made at his factory, Cristallerie Lalique et Cie., in Wingen-sur-Moder, France. From his earliest Coty perfume bottles to the sculptural vases, dishes and plaques inspired by jetting fountains or decorated with graceful female nudes (plate 46), his glass exhibits a precision of workmanship and an attention to detail that have seldom been equaled. Even his radiator ornaments have the quality of small glass sculptures (plate 47). Lalique's influence extended far beyond his own glass company; molded glass objects in Lalique style were produced in a number of other factories in Europe and America.

Maurice Marinot (1882–1960) interrupted his career as a painter to blow glass from about 1911 to 1937 and then returned to painting until his death. During his quarter century as a glassmaker in Troyes, France, Marinot's concept of glass production was similar to that which developed into the Studio Glass Movement in America and Europe in the 1960s. Not only did he design his glass but he actually fabricated each piece "at the fire." His massive vases and bowls combine a strength and sensitivity that exploit the glass medium to the fullest. Bubbles play an important decorative role, and whether the design emphasis is on a limpid fluidity or an icy stability the result is always pleasing.

The exquisite medieval and early Renaissance stained glass and the vital new concepts of the nineteenth and twentieth centuries mark the high points in the development of French artistic glass. When their eighteenth- and nineteenth-century industrial achievements in the production of mirrors and plate glass are added to these artistic accomplishments, it is easy to appreciate the significance of the varied contributions French artists and craftsmen have made to the glassmaking industry.

47

48.
Spanish goblet showing Venetian influence, free-blown in transparent dark blue glass, painted in white enamel and cold-gilt (unfired gilding). Spain, Barcelona, c. 1500. Height: 20.3 cm. (8 in.). Hispanic Society of America, New York

Spain Spanish glass of the sixteenth and seventeenth centuries is a constant delight because of its strong nationalistic designs. The distinctive regional forms with their unrestrained use of rigaree trailings, multiple tubular handles, prunts and pincered accents give the impression that the carefree glassmakers took great delight in producing their exotic creations. Even when the Venetian styles are copied, each piece has a telltale embellishment or change in form which proudly asserts its Spanish origin.

Glass was made in Spain at least as early as the first century A.D. The wares produced from then until about the fourteenth century were similar in many ways to the drinking vessels, cosmetic flasks and other useful products made in other parts of the Roman Empire. As in most areas of central and western Europe, Spanish glassmaking was greatly reduced during the Dark Ages, although there is evidence that it did not cease completely.

In the eleventh and twelfth centuries there were signs of a revival of the industry in the southeastern provinces of Almería and Murcia and in the northeastern area of Catalonia. By the fourteenth century the areas in and around Barcelona had become thriving glassmaking centers, and there were some glassworkers in Palma de Mallorca. The importance of the glassmakers themselves increased in direct proportion to their expanding industry. Political recognition came in the fifteenth century when first one and then two members of the glass guild were given seats on the Barcelona City Council. Each January 1 these enthusiastic artisans held fairs displaying glass from every factory in the area. Stalls filled with glass lined the city streets, and the festival was opened by a gala procession headed by glassmakers and other local dignitaries. Catalan glasswares were not only in great demand locally but by the end of the fifteenth century were famous as far away as Italy, where they were thought by some to rival those of Venice.

During the sixteenth and seventeenth centuries Catalan glassmakers produced their most noteworthy creations. Many were in Venetian styles, usually with a Spanish touch (plate 48), but Islamic influences were also in evidence as were enameled decorations with Mudéjar and Gothic motifs. Royal patronage came in 1503 when Ferdinand purchased 148 handsomely enameled glass pieces for Isabella. A contemporary description indicates these were a superb sampling of the best early sixteenth-century Spanish productions. Made in a variety of colors, the forms ranged from plates, goblets, ewers and basins to covered jars, vases and an impressive *almorratxa* (see plate 49 for an eighteenth-century example of this ceremonial rosewater sprinkler). Later in the century Philip II continued to show royal approval with purchases of Catalan glass recorded in 1564 and again when he visited Barcelona in 1585.

49

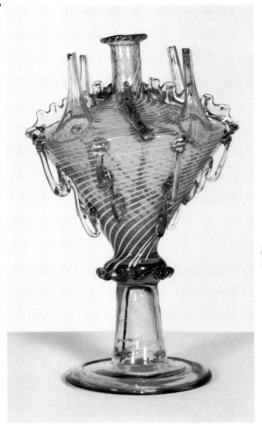

49.
Almorratxa (rosewater sprinkler), a dis-
tinctive Spanish form, free-blown in clear
glass with opaque white spiral threading.
Spain, Catalonia, eighteenth century.
Height: 23.2 cm. (9⅛ in.). Hispanic
Society of America, New York

50.
Free-blown vase of transparent green
glass, with eight applied handles, thread-
ing and pincered tooling. Spain, probably
Almería province, sixteenth century.
Height: 18.8 cm. (7⅜ in.). Metropolitan
Museum of Art, New York, bequest of
Edward G. Moore, 1891

51.
Vase with pattern-molded ribbing blown
from milk white glass and ornamented
with applied pincered and tooled handles
in exuberant Spanish style. Spain, late
seventeenth–early eighteenth century.
Height: 17 cm. (6⅝ in.). Corning Museum of Glass, Corning, N.Y.

50

51

Colorplate 20.
The flamboyant eighteenth-century Catalan cantir (left) contrasts with the more conservative forms of the covered jug and two-handled jar made at the royal factory, La Granja de San Ildefonso, about 1775. All show the Spanish love for ornamentation. Height of covered jug: 32.5 cm. (12¾ in.). Corning Museum of Glass, Corning, N.Y.

52.
Pocket glass, typical of regional designs made by local glassworkers. Free-blown of dark green transparent glass containing seeds and bubbles. Applied handles, threading and pincered chain border. Spain, Maria (Almería), early seventeenth century. Height: 10.2 cm. (4 in.). Collection Jerome Strauss, State College, Penna.

53.
Sugar bowl and cover. Free-blown of clear colorless glass with engraved and gilded floral spray, typical of the style produced by the Spanish royal factory, La Granja de San Ildefonso, c. 1775. Height: 25.5 cm. (10 in.). Hispanic Society of America, New York

Clear colorless glass, sometimes tinged with yellow or gray and made in *façon de Venise* styles, became popular in the sixteenth century. Greenish shades were also prevalent. Multihandled vases with elaborate tooling and threadings were a typical Spanish innovation (plate 50). Venetian influence continued well into the eighteenth century, always with Spanish embellishments (colorplate 20). As in other European glass centers, milk white glass was produced, but in typical Spanish glass forms that continued the use of applied handles, often in extravagant loopings (plate 51). Glass made in Catalonia and elsewhere during the nineteenth century is more plentiful but usually less appealing to collectors than the sixteenth- and seventeenth-century productions.

The glass centers in Andalusia were the most consistent in producing their distinctive national styles. These were chiefly vases, flasks and drinking vessels made in transparent leaf and olive greens, greenish blues and smoky yellows. The colors were, for the most part, due to impurities in the glass batch. Quality control was nonexistent, but the seeds, bubbles and striae common in these glasses served to enhance rather than detract from their charm (plate 52).

The establishment of the royal factory, La Granja de San Ildefonso, near Segovia, in 1728 tended to decrease the importance of glass productions in other Spanish factories. For decades the priority products of the factory were large plate-glass mirrors for the palaces of Philip

52

53

V, Charles III and Charles IV, who added the crystal chandeliers which still adorn the palaces in Madrid and Aranjuez. From about the mid-eighteenth century, glassmakers and engravers brought from France, Sweden and other countries assisted in producing the clear colorless glass (often tinged with green or yellow) that was usually decorated with floral sprays in gilded engraving (plate 53) or painted in gold directly on the glass. Covered jugs and jars with engraved and enameled decorations were also made, sometimes with tooled finials (see colorplate 20). These hand-blown wares are still available to collectors at fairly reasonable prices and are more plentiful than the blue glass with splashed or hooked decorations in opaque white made about the same time. Even in the 1760s the factory was becoming too great a luxury for its royal patrons. In spite of numerous attempts through the last decades of the eighteenth century and the early years of the nineteenth to make the works solvent, they were finally leased to a private company in 1829.

Beginning in the nineteenth century, Spanish glassmaking became more industrialized and glassmaking facilities expanded to include mass-produced commercial wares. These productions as well as ornamental glass and tablewares continue to compare favorably with similar wares made elsewhere in Europe, and at times are reminiscent of early regional designs.

Scandinavia and Finland   Glassmaking in Scandinavia began when German glassworkers were brought to Denmark in 1550 to make glass for the king. These workmen set up small glasshouses in the forests of East Jutland and continued to make a limited amount of glass until about 1660, when the factories were forced to close because the supply of wood fuel was exhausted. For the next 150 years, when no glass was being made in Denmark, all glasswares were imported, first from glass centers in central Europe and from the 1740s to about 1808 from Norway.

In the nineteenth century no significant amount of glass was produced in Denmark until after 1825, when the Holmegaards Glassworks was established at Fensmark, about fifty miles southwest of Copenhagen. This location was chosen because of the ample supply of peat fuel. By the 1840s the factory was flourishing and since the mid-nineteenth century has produced bottles and a wide variety of free-blown and mold-blown tablewares mostly in English and Continental styles. In 1847 Holmegaards built the Kastrup Glassworks, near Copenhagen, to take over its bottle production. It sold this glasshouse in 1873, and from then on tablewares were made at both factories. In 1965 the factories again combined and have operated since as Kastrup and Holmegaards Glassworks, Ltd. Much of Holmegaards's best glass has been made in the twentieth century, when fine individual designers have been allowed to use the factory facilities

54.
Strong Venetian influences are evident in the form and intricately tooled and applied decorations on this handsome presentation goblet, free-blown from clear colorless glass, now with some crizzling. The *CE* monograms of Charles XI and Ulrika Eleonora of Sweden were incorporated in the stem decorations. Kungsholm Glass Factory, near Stockholm, Sweden, before 1693. Height overall: 46 cm. (18⅛ in.). Corning Museum of Glass, Corning, N.Y.

to make their own special pieces or have designed the firm's commercial wares.

In 1571, about two decades after German glassmakers came to Denmark, a glasshouse in Hälsingborg, Sweden, was started with the assistance of Venetian artisans. This attempt was short-lived, but in 1676 another group of glassmakers from Murano helped to establish the Kungsholm Glass Factory, near Stockholm, and continued to influence its productions for the next two decades (plate 54). Shortly before 1700 the Kungsholm factory began emulating German and Bohemian styles and from the 1690s until it closed in 1815 produced a great deal of fine glass, including a number of elegant covered *Pokale* for presentation pieces.

The oldest glass factory still in operation in Sweden is the Kosta Glassworks. Founded in 1792 to make window glass, it soon expanded its production to include drinking glasses and chandeliers and has continued to be an outstanding contributor to the present preeminence of the Swedish glass industry. Boda Glassworks, founded in 1864, has gained its greatest fame in the twentieth century. Its molded-glass elements, combined with iron and other metals in chandeliers and candlesticks, and its heavy free-blown crystal glass bowls and vases with deep intaglio engraving were particularly successful. Another Swedish factory, Orrefors Glassworks, founded in 1898, also owes its prominence to its twentieth-century productions. From about 1916, under the leadership of Simon Gate and Edward Hald, the company achieved fame for its fine wheel-engraved wares and the highly technical and artistic achievements in Ariel, Graal, Kraka and Ravenna glasses. The productions of Orrefors greatly influenced glassmaking in a number of European and American factories. This can be noted in ornamental glass made during the second quarter of the twentieth century, particularly during the 1930s.

Glassmaking in Norway began in 1741 at the Nøstetangen Glass Factory, which made tablewares and chandeliers mostly for the Norwegian and Danish markets. In 1777 the Hurdals Glassworks took over these productions and continued to supply Norway and Denmark until about 1808, when the Danish-Norwegian kingdom came to an end. Meanwhile the Hadelands Glassworks, which was to become Norway's most important glasshouse, was established in 1762 and operated for the next ninety years primarily as a bottle factory. In the 1850s Hadelands was acquired by the Berg family, which expanded its productions to include fine ornamental pieces and tablewares in crystal and colored glass. This factory has continued to dominate Norwegian glass production until the present day.

Glassmaking was practiced briefly in Finland in the late seventeenth century at a factory in Nystad which operated from 1631 to 1685. During the eighteenth century the industry achieved more stability under Swedish glassmakers, producing mostly commercial wares.

Since the 1920s three Finnish factories have attained prominence in the production of fine artistic and commercial glass: Notsjö Glassworks, founded in 1793; Iittala Glassworks (now using the trade name Arabia), established in 1881; and Riihimäki, started in 1910.

Russia   There is evidence that glass was made in Russia as early as the third century A.D. Excavations in the Ukraine disclose the remains of glasshouses and fragments of colorless and greenish wares similar to those made in many parts of the Roman Empire. By the early eighteenth century considerable glassmaking was under way in a number of private and state-owned factories scattered in many areas from Leningrad to Kiev. Most of their better free-blown tablewares were made for the czar and the nobility in fine clear colorless glass with wheel-engraved monograms, imperial insignia or medallions of saints (plate 55). Less expensive wares were usually in greenish and colorless glass with painted enamel decorations. From about 1750 rich ruby reds, deep blues, violets and emerald greens with painted gilding were popular. There was also some experimental work in mosaics, *Zwischengoldglas* and opaque white wares painted in porcelain styles.

Some of the most distinguished Russian glass was made in the first half of the nineteenth century at the Imperial Glass Factory in St. Petersburg. This included fine cut crystal decanters and other tablewares often bearing inscriptions commemorating Russian victories over Napoleon. But by far the most spectacular objects were a number of monumental urns and vases, some over four feet high, composed of crystal with red or blue glass casings and deep-cut designs (plate 56). There were also pieces of furniture and fountains with glass components set in ormolu (gilt bronze) mounts. These were made for palaces in Russia and abroad (plate 58).

The privately owned concerns made no attempt to rival the Imperial Glass Factory in these large-scale productions, but several competed very favorably in other areas of luxury glassmaking. One of these, the Bakhmetev Glassworks, founded in 1763 at Nikolskoe, Penza, produced, in addition to its more conventional wares, an unusual group of double-walled beakers in the early nineteenth century. Between the walls of these beakers were miniature landscapes with goats, fishermen and an island cottage made of straw, moss and paper. These glasses have survived amazingly well considering the fragility of the materials involved (plate 57). Another important factory, Gus-Krustalny, founded in 1756, gained prominence in the eighteenth century for its useful and decorative wares. This glasshouse received gold medals for its crystal glass in the First All-Russian Exhibition in 1829. It has maintained its eighteenth- and nineteenth-century standards and become especially noted in the twentieth century for its colored tablewares, blown ornamental figures and cut and engraved pieces styled by its talented artist-designers.

55.
Free-blown covered *Pokal* in Bohemian style with facet-cut stem and wheel-engraved decorations, including a medallion of Saint Andereas. Russia, eighteenth century. Height: 40.8 cm. (16 in.). Smithsonian Institution, National Museum of History and Technology

56.
Monumental urn and pedestal mold-blown in three sections of clear colorless glass with a dark blue casing, and assembled after the cut decorations were completed. Imperial Glass Factory, St. Petersburg, Russia, c. 1830. Height: 70.1 cm. (27⅝ in.). Hillwood, Washington, D.C.

57.
Extremely rare double-walled beaker of clear colorless glass with pastoral scenes, made of straw, moss and paper, enclosed between the walls. Outer surface ornamented with cut vertical panel flutings and painted gold border of oak leaves and acorns. Bakhmetev Glassworks, Nikolskoe, Penza, Russia, c. 1820. Height: 14.7 cm. (5¾ in.). Smithsonian Institution, National Collection of Fine Arts, gift of John Gellatly

58.
Table of blue and amber glass with bronze and ormolu mounts. Imperial Glass Factory, St. Petersburg, Russia, after a design by A. N. Voronikhin, c. 1804. Height: 79 cm. (31⅛ in.). Corning Museum of Glass, Corning, N.Y.

55

56

57

58

In spite of unfavorable economic conditions in the mid-nineteenth century, Russian glassmakers took part in the revival of Gothic, Byzantine, Chinese and other traditional styles which had begun in England after the Great Exhibition of 1851. Renaissance and rococo decorations were also brought back and a new regional style called "Russian" made its appearance. This style imitated peasant wood and metal objects in glass and is intriguing to collectors of unusual glass. Pressed glass was also made, and toward the close of the century "brilliant" cut glass and Art Nouveau styles achieved considerable popularity.

England and Ireland   England can trace its earliest glass to the period of the Roman occupation. Excavations of Roman glass-factory sites indicate that flasks, bowls and other common wares were produced in Britain, but they are so similar to those made in other parts of the Roman Empire that many could have been brought in by the invaders. After the Romans withdrew from Britain, glassmaking was reduced to continuations of the simpler Roman forms made mostly in yellowish or greenish glass of medium to poor quality. Anglo-Saxon graves of the fifth to seventh centuries have yielded a variety of pouch bottles and palm cups as well as some claw beakers and the rare drinking horns. The more complicated forms, particularly the claw beaker (see plate 15), are found as often on the Continent as in England, but the pouch bottles are found almost exclusively in England, in and around Kent, and so are thought to be of English origin.

The present English glass industry had its somewhat modest beginnings in the thirteenth century, when window-glass makers from Normandy established their crown glass factories in Kent, Sussex and Surrey. The sixteenth century saw the arrival of more French window-glass makers, this time from Lorraine, who settled in the areas of Stourbridge and Newcastle-upon-Tyne. These workmen used the more efficient cylinder, or broad, glass method of production and brought new life to the English flat-glass industry, which has continued with outstanding success to the present day.

During the fifteenth and sixteenth centuries everyday glasswares were made in the English window-glass factories, but the finer glass was imported from the Continent. Sales of these imports and management of the factories were largely controlled by promoters, who obtained the "privileges" to set up glass factories and brought in workers to staff them. In the 1550s the government exerted pressure on these promoters to expand the manufacture of English tablewares and thus decrease the demand for imported glass. With this objective, one of the promoters, Jean Carré, established a factory at Crutched Friars, London, about 1571, to make Venetian-style glassware and staffed it with Venetian workmen. Among these glassmakers was Jacopo Verzelini, who had been a successful glassmaker in Antwerp since the 1550s. After Carré's death in 1572, Verzelini stayed on as manager of the Crutched Friars glasshouse until it burned a year or two later. About 1574 he built another glasshouse in London and obtained a twenty-one-year privilege from Queen Elizabeth I to make glass in the Venetian style. From then on he apparently prospered, as he retired an esteemed glassmaker and a wealthy man in 1592.

Several of Verzelini's delicate *façon de Venise* goblets still exist. The earliest known has a hunting scene and the date 1577 surrounded by foliate motifs. Most of them seem to have been made as special orders. Their diamond-engraved decorations in the sixteenth-century Venetian style include monograms, dates and appropriate inscriptions (plate 59). After Verzelini's retirement his successors in London and other English glasshouses continued to produce *façon de Venise* glassware, which was fashionable in England for most of the seventeenth century.

In spite of the better tablewares made by Verzelini and his successors, England continued to import large quantities of Venetian glass. The course of English glassmaking continued to be charted by monopolistic promoters, notably Sir Robert Mansell, a retired admiral. He controlled the importation and manufacture of everything made of glass, from windowpanes and mirrors to vials and tablewares, for almost twenty-five years. After Mansell's monopoly ended in 1640, the Glass-Sellers' Company of London emerged as the important importers of Venetian wares, which were made in Murano after designs sent from London. Endless arguments over mistakes in filling orders and breakage during shipping emphasized the desirability of having more glass made in England. The main obstacle to this was the quality of the English glass, which was still inferior to Venetian *cristallo*. To remedy this the Glass-Sellers' Company engaged George Ravenscroft, a noted glassmaking authority, for the specific purpose of improving the quality of English clear colorless glass. When they gave him this commission in 1674, they could not have foreseen that within two years he was to perfect, at his Savoy glasshouse in London, a lead-glass formula destined to be the greatest improvement in the quality of clear colorless glass since the Venetian perfection of *cristallo*. In addition to the impetus this new lead-glass formula gave artistic glass and fine tablewares, it had a tremendous effect on the production of optical glass. The development of microscopes, telescopes and the like would have been impossible, or at least completely different, without Ravenscroft's invention of a glass with totally new optical qualities.

Ravenscroft's own designs are distinctive, often having much of their surfaces covered by a diamond-shaped relief pattern which he called *nipt diamond waies* (plate 60). After his lead-glass formula was perfected, he was allowed to mark his pieces with a prunt bearing a raven's head (plate 61). Although Anglo-Venetian styles continued for some years after Ravenscroft's glass was adopted by most English factories,

59.
Venetian-style goblet, free-blown in clear slightly brownish glass with a diamond-point engraved frieze of animals above a border of floral motifs encircling the goblet's bowl. The monogram *AT* appears on the obverse; the date *1578*, on the reverse. Made by Jacopo Verzelini, London, England, 1578. Height: 21 cm. (8¼ in.). Fitzwilliam Museum, Cambridge, England

60

61

60.

Decanter jug, free-blown of clear colorless lead glass. The overall decoration of
nipt diamond waies and pincered vertical
ribs is typical of Ravenscroft's designs.
The fine crizzling indicates it may have
been one of his experimental pieces made
before his lead-glass formula was fully
perfected in or about 1676. England,
1670s. Height: 20.7 cm. (8⅛ in.). Smithsonian Institution, National Museum of
History and Technology

61.

Posset pot, free-blown in lead glass with
applied spout, handles and gadrooned
base. The raven's-head seal, applied to
the base of the spout, indicates this piece
was made after Ravenscroft perfected his
lead-glass formula. George Ravenscroft's
Savoy Glasshouse, London, late 1670s.
Height: 11.5 cm. (4½ in.). Fitzwilliam
Museum, Cambridge, England

the beauty of the lead crystal fostered the development of a style which
accented form rather than applied decorations. These late seventeenth-
and early eighteenth-century goblets and wineglasses with their massive
baluster stems, acorn knops and graceful conical bowls form a group
of tablewares whose elegant beauty has seldom been equaled. After the
heavy balusters and knops had been in fashion for some decades the
so-called *Silesian stem* appeared. This molded stem usually had four or
six ribbed panels tapering downward from a rounded shoulder. Later
the shoulder was often ornamented with molded diamonds and sometimes surmounted with molded inscriptions (plate 62). While this
form of stem was probably made in Silesia, it actually originated in
the Hessian region of Germany. Its acceptance in England was an
indication of the change in attitude toward German influences after
the Treaty of Utrecht in 1713.

About 1735 the *air-twist stem* (plate 63), an English innovation, was
developed from the earlier teardrop, or bubble, stem. The success of
this stem was soon supplemented by the *opaque twists* (plate 64),
which virtually dominated wineglass productions from the late 1740s
to the 1760s. These twists were an adaptation of the Venetian filigree,
or *latticino*, technique in which spiraled opaque white and/or colored
threadings were encased in clear colorless glass. The threadings were
intertwined, swirled and sometimes combined with air twists to form

a myriad of fascinating spirals. Their descriptive names, gauze twist, lacy twist, double opaque twist, corkscrew twist and mixed twist, suggest a few of the almost endless variations which attracted buyers at the time and have intrigued collectors ever since. Opaque twists were used to ornament a host of tablewares as well as candelabra, vases and other ornamental objects. They supplemented the other glass table accessories such as salts, finger bowls and wineglass coolers or rinsers (plate 65).

Opaque white glass was used in England, as on the Continent, to imitate porcelain. Preferred forms were oviform vases, tapersticks and covered jars painted in polychrome floral arrangements and other designs by artists in the Midlands, London and the Bristol area from the 1760s to the early 1800s (plate 66). Although only a few glass pieces can be tentatively attributed to Michael Edkins (1734–1811), he is the best-known artist of the Bristol area who painted these porcelain-type pieces. His fame is due as much to the survival of his detailed work records as to the fine quality of his painting.

A more original style of enameled decoration in opaque colors was being done about the same time in Newcastle-upon-Tyne by two members of the Beilby family. William Beilby (1740–1819) and his sister, Mary (1749–1797), painted superb armorial designs and rustic

62.
Wineglass in clear colorless glass with Silesian stem having a molded inscription, "God Bless King George." England, eighteenth century. Height: 17.8 cm. (7 in.). Fitzwilliam Museum, Cambridge, England

63.
Wineglass free-blown in lead-crystal glass with air-twist stem, an eighteenth-century English innovation. England, mid-eighteenth century. Height: 19 cm. (7½ in.). Smithsonian Institution, National Museum of History and Technology, Clara W. Berwick Collection

62

63

64.
Privateer glasses, so called because they were decorated with engravings of privately owned armed sailing ships. All have opaque-twist stems. England, mid-eighteenth century. Height of each: about 15.3 cm. (6 in.). Fitzwilliam Museum, Cambridge, England

65.
Wineglass cooler or rinser, mold-blown with cut and engraved decorations. First used in England in the late seventeenth century, such vessels were designed to hold ice water for cooling or rinsing wineglasses by diners while at table. Free-blown wineglass with opaque-twist stem is shown in rinser. Both England, eighteenth century. Height of rinser: 9.1 cm. (3½ in.). Wineglass, Collection Mr. and Mrs. Thomas L. Wolf, New York. Rinser, Cooper-Hewitt Museum, gift of Mr. and Mrs. Arthur Wiesenberger

64

Colorplate 21.
Free-blown lead-glass goblets with opaque-twist stems and splendid enamel decorations painted by William and Mary Beilby. The goblet on the left has the coat of arms of Pembroke and Montgomery and is signed *Beilby*. England, Newcastle-upon-Tyne, c. 1760–70. Height of tallest goblet: 22.7 cm. (8⅞ in.). Corning Museum of Glass, Corning, N.Y.

landscapes with rococo embellishments usually on clear colorless glass goblets (colorplate 21), decanters and other tablewares made in the Newcastle area. These artists worked from about 1762 to 1778, and their signed pieces are highly prized by museums and collectors. The area also produced fine crystal-glass blanks that were sold to decorators in other parts of England and on the Continent or were decorated locally by enamelers or engravers (plate 67).

A natural use of the brilliant reflective and refractive lead crystal was for chandeliers and other lighting accessories. At first, lead crystal was used just for pendants on the metal frames of chandeliers; then, by the 1740s all-glass arms, candle cups and bobeches were in vogue. Toward the end of the century, forms and decorations became more elaborate (see frontispiece), and the Regency and Victorian periods saw even more extravagances involving clusters of prismatic pendants and cascades of graduated drops with gemlike cuttings. Chandeliers and lighting devices such as candelabra, sconces and candlesticks have continued to be a delightful part of English and Irish glass productions.

The Glass Excise Tax levied in 1745 on the weight of materials used by glassmakers in England caused significant changes in glass formulas and designs. Manufacturers decreased the amounts of lead in the glass batch, made existing shapes thinner and adopted the lighter rococo

66.
Tapersticks and covered jar in opaque white glass with painted decorations in polychrome enamels imitating porcelain. England, Bristol, c. 1770. Height of jar: 21 cm. (8¼ in.). Fitzwilliam Museum, Cambridge, England

forms which had been popular on the Continent since the 1720s. When free trade with Ireland was granted in 1780, English glassmakers and promoters lost no time in founding factories there, often with English workmen. Heavy blanks suitable for cutting, which were brought tax free to England for local sale or export, constituted a major portion of these Irish productions. This collaboration became less profitable when Ireland levied a Glass Excise Tax in 1825. Then when the English Glass Excise Tax was repealed in 1845, the Anglo-Irish glass era came to an end.

Among the best-known Irish glasshouses of the Anglo-Irish period were the Waterford Glass House and the Cork Glass Company, both established in 1783, and Charles Mulvaney & Company, Dublin, in 1785. Waterford, a name which has come to be synonymous with fine Irish glass, produced some of the world's most beautiful cut and engraved glass until it closed in 1851 (plate 68). Exactly a century later, 1951, the Waterford factory reopened and has continued to make fine quality cut lead-crystal glass, mostly in traditional patterns, until the present day.

Most eighteenth- and nineteenth-century Irish glass is unmarked (plate 69), except for a few mold-blown decanters having *Cork Glass Co., Penrose Waterford* or *CM & Co.* imprinted on their bases. The unmarked bluish gray cut-glass pieces, particularly the boat-shaped footed bowls, formerly attributed to Waterford, are now thought to have been made at Cork or some other contemporary Irish glasshouse.

The nineteenth century was a period of great activity and expansion in the English glassmaking industry. Technical advances were particularly apparent. The adoption of the American process for machine-pressing of glass in the 1830s was followed as the century progressed by the invention of numerous machines for threading, making air-trap patterns, simulating dragged decorations and performing many other shaping and decorating processes formerly done by hand. The vitality of the industrial community in midcentury was symbolized by the Great Exhibition of 1851 held in the vast Crystal Palace erected in London's Hyde Park. The fact that the glass panes for this spectacular structure were all blown by hand by the cylinder method, with the entire project being completed and installed in less than a year, is as impressive as the multitude of wares it eventually housed. Among these wares were huge chandeliers twenty feet in height and half as large in diameter, which vied with a twenty-seven-foot glass fountain as the most eye-catching extravagances of the exhibition. Later in the century the Philadelphia Centennial Exposition and the Paris exhibitions of 1878 and 1889 continued to give international exposure to English glass productions.

Among the items offered at fairs and exhibitions were glass novelties of all kinds, including fascinating glass miniatures. Whether they were designed specifically for dollhouse furnishings or as amusing toys, they

67.
Commemorative goblet in free-blown lead-crystal glass with opaque-twist stem. Wheel-engraved decoration depicting John Wilkes holding the "Bill of Rights." England, probably Newcastle-upon-Tyne, c. 1760. Height: 29.2 cm. (11½ in.). Smithsonian Institution, National Museum of History and Technology

68.
Fine cut glass in Irish patterns which
have become traditional and have inspired
productions in contemporary glassmaking
centers on the Continent and in America.
Probably Waterford Glass House, Waterford, Ireland, first half of the nineteenth
century. Height of decanter and stopper:
38.4 cm. (15⅛ in.). Cooper-Hewitt Museum, gift of the Misses Hewitt (water
glass) and bequest of Mrs. John Innes
Kane

69.
Pitcher blown in deep blue glass, an unusual color, with applied handle and cut
decorations. Ireland, c. 1820. Height:
17.5 cm. (6⅞ in.). Cooper-Hewitt Museum

70.
Miniature glass tablewares perhaps made
for dollhouse furnishings. The tea set is
blue, the candlestick has a blue candle
cup and opaque-twist stem and the cruet
set and wineglasses are in clear colorless
glass. England, probably Bristol, mid-
nineteenth century. Height of candlestick: 4.5 cm. (1¾ in.). Cooper-Hewitt
Museum, gift of Hamill and Barker

68

69

were made in all kinds of glassmaking processes from pressing and blowing to lampworking (plate 70) and continue to delight their owners whether they reside in palaces or cottages.

Among the important glasshouses that contributed to the success of the English glass industry in the eighteenth and nineteenth centuries and that have continued to maintain their high standards is Whitefriars, which operated in London from about 1680 to 1923, when it moved to Wealdstone, Middlesex. Long noted for its tablewares, during the last 150 years it has also been known for its stained glass, glasses copied from museum specimens, *millefiori* paperweights and other decorative objects. Pilkington Brothers, Ltd., in St. Helens, Lancashire, since about 1826, is one of the world's largest producers of industrial flat and plate glass. It is especially noted for its perfection, in 1959, of the *float-glass process* for producing plate glass. In this process a continuous ribbon of molten glass is pulled across a bath of liquid tin at a controlled temperature. This ingenious manipulation produces a con-

70

71

tinuous sheet of plate glass which can be cut into panes as it emerges from the cooling oven and is ready for merchandising without the expensive grinding and polishing necessary in other processes. The Pilkington firm established and still maintains a fine museum in their factory complex at St. Helens, which shows the history and techniques of glassmaking and is supplemented by a fine collection of glass objects.

Paralleling the mass production and mechanization advances during the last half of the nineteenth century was a resurgence of interest in the revival of ancient glassmaking styles and techniques. In the Stourbridge area Thomas Webb & Sons, which operated under various ownerships in the nineteenth century, was especially noted for its late nineteenth-century cameo (plate 71) and rock-crystal glass engraved by William Fritsche, Frederick Kny and Franz Joseph Palme. Stevens & Williams, which began as the Moor Lane Glass House in the mid-eighteenth century, was famous during the late nineteenth and early twentieth centuries for its art glass, sometimes using Venetian techniques (plate 72).

It was John Northwood I, a Stourbridge artist, who had sparked this renewed interest in ancient glassmaking styles when he copied the famous Portland Vase during the years 1873 to 1876. Northwood's masterpiece is the Pegasus Vase (plate 73), which he completed in 1882 after six years of work. Other artists who carved outstanding cameo glass were Joseph Locke, George and Thomas Woodall, Frederick Carder, John Northwood II, Alphonse Lechevrel and other contemporaries and pupils of John Northwood I. The Woodalls,

72

71.
Cameo glass vase with blue body cased in opaque white and pink layers, which were cut through to produce the elegant floral decorations in Persian style. Thomas Webb & Sons, Stourbridge, England, c. 1880. Height: 46.5 cm. (18¼ in.). Royal Ontario Museum, Toronto

72.
Bowl, free-blown in lace glass, a technique the Venetians called *vetro a reticello* (network glass). In this technique, skillful manipulations by the glassblower enclosed a network of bubbles between opaque white threads crisscrossed and enclosed in clear colorless glass. Probably made by Stevens & Williams, Brierley Hill, England, late nineteenth century. Height: 11.5 cm. (4½ in.). Smithsonian Institution, National Museum of History and Technology, Clara W. Berwick Collection

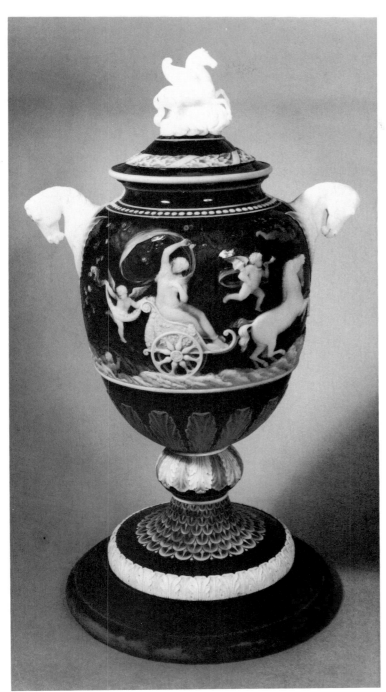

73.
The Pegasus Vase. Cameo glass, opaque white cased over dark blue with carved relief decorations depicting Aurora in her chariot on one side and Aphrodite with her attendants on the other. The cover finial is a sculptured glass statuette of Pegasus. Carved by John Northwood I between 1876 and 1882 and signed by him. England, Stourbridge, dated 1882. Height: 54.6 cm. (21½ in.). Smithsonian Institution, National Collection of Fine Arts, gift of John Gellatly

George especially, created some of the most detailed carved cameo glass ever produced.

England's greatest single contribution to eighteenth- and nineteenth-century glassmaking was undoubtedly the perfection and exploitation of the lead-glass formula. But the continuing vitality and high standards of quality maintained over the years by the English glass industry have also earned it worldwide recognition for its artistic and commercial glasswares.

4 Glass in the New World

Glassmaking in the New World had inauspicious beginnings. Two short-lived attempts were made in the early seventeenth century, both at Jamestown, Virginia. The first was in 1608, sponsored by the London Company, with eight German and Polish workmen. It failed within a year. The second, started in 1621, this time with Italian glassblowers, lasted a frustrating fourteen months, but was no more successful than the earlier venture. Other seventeenth-century factories existed for undetermined periods in Salem, Massachusetts, New Amsterdam and Philadelphia, but all failed to gain a firm foothold for the glassmaking industry in America.

Late in 1739 Caspar Wistar opened what was to be the New World's first successful glasshouse at a site, now often called Wistarberg, located about eight miles southwest of Salem, New Jersey. In 1717 Wistar had come from Germany to Philadelphia, where he operated a successful brass-button factory before deciding to make window glass and bottles. Apparently his judgment concerning glass was as good as it had been about brass buttons, for his glass factory stayed in business forty years, a record for colonial glasshouses. His success was due in part to his selection of a factory site near ample supplies of sand for the glass batch and wood for fuel. It was also near Philadelphia and accessible to water transportation. Since he had no practical glassmaking knowledge, he had brought four glassmakers from the Low Countries to southern New Jersey in December, 1738, to teach him and his workmen how to make glass.

From the start, production was concentrated on window glass and bottles, usually in shades of amber and olive green. Although these staples of the glass industry kept Wistar's factory going, the fame of South Jersey glass today rests on the free-blown sugar bowls, candlesticks, milkpans and other household items made from the factory's common window and bottle glass (colorplate 23). While a limited number of these pieces may have been made for sale by the factory,

Colorplate 22.
Louis Comfort Tiffany's Art Nouveau and other decorative glass styles were the finest produced anywhere. These free-blown Favrile vases were made at Tiffany Furnaces, Corona, Long Island, New York, late nineteenth–early twentieth century. Height of tallest vase: 46 cm. (18 in.). Cooper-Hewitt Museum, **gifts** (from the left) of Harry Harkness Flagler; Thomas Carnase; and Stanley Siegel from the collection of Stanley Siegel. Vase at right, purchase in memory of Georgiana L. McClellan

Colorplate 23.
The free-blown candlesticks and sugar
bowl, some of the earliest-known pieces
of American glass, may have been made
at the Wistar factory, 1740–80. Mug with
white loopings made at the Isabella Glass
Works, c. 1850. Threaded mug and gemel
bottle also made in eighteenth or nineteenth century but factory is unknown.
All are New Jersey glass. Height of
candlesticks: 19.2 cm. (7½ in.). Corning
Museum of Glass, Corning, N.Y.

Colorplate 24.
The pattern-molded pitcher, pocket flask and sugar bowl and the engraved mug and enamel-painted beaker are typical of the first fine glass made in America by Henry William Stiegel. Unless documented, these pieces are called Stiegel-type. The enameled inscription on the beaker reads, "My love you Like me do." Probably Manheim, Pennsylvania, 1765–74. Height of mug: 15.7 cm. (6⅛ in.). Corning Museum of Glass, Corning, N.Y.

most were probably blown for the glassworkers' families or friends. The charm of these household items lies in their straightforward functional forms, often embellished with applied threadings, rigaree trailings and the now-famous lily-pad decorations. These pieces, which the German glassmakers might have made in their homeland, established in America the Germanic glassmaking tradition that was to continue well into the nineteenth century. After Wistar died in 1752 his son, Richard, carried on the business successfully until 1780.

In 1781 the Stanger (or Stenger) brothers, former Wistar employees, established the second New Jersey glassworks at Glassboro in Gloucester County. Although their proprietorship ended in 1784, the Glassboro factory continued under a succession of owners well into the twentieth century.

New Jersey glassmaking expanded considerably in the nineteenth century with about forty factories operating for varying lengths of time between the 1820s and the 1880s. In 1806 James Lee founded a factory in Millville which, after various ownerships, became Whitall, Tatum & Company in 1857 (later a division of Armstrong Cork). From about 1863 this factory and several others in the area became famous for their paperweights, especially the Millville Rose made by at least four South Jersey gaffers in the early twentieth century.

Another important Millville glasshouse, T. C. Wheaton & Company, was founded in 1888 to make bottles and tubing. This successful enterprise, now Wheaton Industries and still controlled by the Wheaton family, has become one of America's largest producers of pressed and blown containers, tablewares, novelties and other glass specialties. In Millville the company maintains a fine glass museum in a restored nineteenth-century South Jersey town called Victorian Wheaton Village. There, in a replica of Wheaton's nineteenth-century glasshouse, visitors can see glassblowing and purchase productions of the factory and independent studio artists.

As early as the 1760s New Jersey's glassmaking activities were being supplemented by those in an area across the state line in southeastern Pennsylvania. This area became an important glassmaking center from 1763 to 1774, thanks to the ambitions of a young German immigrant named Henry William Stiegel. Probably no other eighteenth-century American glassmaker has captivated the fancy of historians and glass collectors to a greater degree than has Stiegel. This enterprising young German arrived in Philadelphia in 1750 at the age of twenty-one. Within two years he had found employment in the ironworks of Jacob Huber and had married Elizabeth Huber, the daughter of this prominent Lancaster County, Pennsylvania, ironmaker. By the time Stiegel was twenty-nine he had been made a partner in his father-in-law's ironworks, fathered two daughters, become a widower, remarried and acquired another iron foundry.

But being a successful ironmaker and solid citizen was not enough to satisfy this ambitious young man. He became fascinated with glass. With typical enthusiasm he established three glasshouses in quick succession in Lancaster County—the first, at Elizabeth Furnace, in 1763; the second, at Manheim, in 1765; and the third, another Manheim glasshouse, in 1769. This last one he called the American Flint Glass Works and staffed with English and Continental workmen. Everything went well at first. Stiegel's glassblowers turned out handsome pattern-molded sugar bowls, salts and pocket bottles in gleaming flint-glass blues, emerald greens and amethyst colors which rivaled the English imports then and thrill collectors today (colorplate 24). In fact, he was so successful in equaling the styles and quality of his foreign competitors that today it is safest to call any undocumented glass which could have been produced at Manheim Stiegel-type.

Unfortunately, Stiegel misjudged the American glass market and overextended his resources. Sales plummeted, and by 1773 he was faced with bankruptcy. Even the sale of his foundries and real-estate holdings could not salvage his enterprise. The glassworks failed in 1774, and Stiegel went to debtor's prison. He was soon released, but his life from then on is not chronicled. He died in 1785 and was buried in an unmarked grave.

After Stiegel's factory closed, no fine glass was made in America for about a decade. The manufacture of better-grade useful and decorative wares was resumed in 1785, when John Frederick Amelung founded the third of the most important eighteenth-century American glasshouses, the New Bremen Glassmanufactory, in Frederick County, Maryland. Like Wistar and Stiegel, Amelung was a native of Germany, but unlike them he was an experienced glassmaker, having managed a mirror and sheet-glass factory in Grünenwald, Germany, with his brother.

He planned his American project carefully before leaving Germany. In addition to the glassmaking facilities, he envisioned a factory town with a church and school in which the workers' children could be taught music as well as German and English. Having obtained a £10,000 capitalization from a group of businessmen in Bremen, Germany, he named his American factory in honor of that city.

On August 31, 1784, Amelung arrived in Baltimore with seven members of his family and sixty-one glassworkers recruited from Bohemia and Germany. Because of his predeparture planning he was soon able to acquire the Foltz glasshouse, a failing manufactory in Frederick County, Maryland, and enough adjoining land to start glass production early in 1785.

During the next few years Amelung's dream project developed rapidly, but in May of 1790 a fire destroyed a warehouse and one of his factories. Sales of his glass declined and he was plagued with

74.
This covered goblet, called the *Bremen Pokal*, was one of the earliest engraved presentation glasses made in America. Free-blown of nonlead slightly greenish glass, it was made for Amelung's German backers and sent to Bremen, Germany, about 1788. The wheel-engraved decoration shows the arms of the city of Bremen. The inscriptions read, "Old Bremen Success and the New Progress" (obverse) and "New Bremen Glassmanufactory 1788 North America State of Maryland" (reverse). New Bremen Glassmanufactory, 1788. Height: 28.5 cm. (11¼ in.). Metropolitan Museum of Art, New York, Rogers Fund, 1928

75.
The "W.A.G." tumblers may have been wedding gifts for Abigail Angell and William Austin Goddard, who were married about 1790. They were free-blown in nonlead glass with yellowish brown tints (covered pair) and grayish tinges (center tumbler). New Bremen Glassmanufactory, Maryland, c. 1790. Height of covered tumblers: 30.2 cm. (11⅞ in.). Smithsonian Institution, National Museum of History and Technology

75

76.
The swan finial and applied handles with pincered trailings on this sugar bowl, which was free-blown of clear greenish yellow glass, are similar to some found on glass produced at Amelung's factory. Since its origin is undocumented, it is tentatively attributed to either the New Bremen or the New Geneva factory, late eighteenth or early nineteenth century. Height: 20.7 cm. (8⅛ in.). Smithsonian Institution, National Museum of History and Technology

76

production difficulties. A stroke which Amelung suffered in 1794 signaled the end of his enterprise, and the factory was put up for sale in March of 1795. Amelung died on November 1, 1798.

Although the New Bremen Glassmanufactory lasted only a decade, it marked a major chapter in the history of American glassmaking if only because of its engraved presentation pieces. All of these are free-blown of clear nonlead glass and vary considerably in glass quality. Some have tinges of green, brown or gray, as in his common wares, and a number have stones, bubbles and cords. But the engraving is outstanding today and was the finest produced in America up to that time (plates 74 and 75). Fewer than fifty of these engraved pieces have been positively identified as having been made at Amelung's factory. Many others, both plain and engraved, which were previously thought to have a New Bremen origin, are now being reevaluated in the light of recent research.

The Midwest Glass was first produced west of the Allegheny Mountains in January, 1798, by the New Geneva Glass Works, New Geneva, Pennsylvania. This factory was actually begun in 1797 by a group of glassmakers with the help of Albert Gallatin, then a congressman and later Secretary of the Treasury under Presidents Jefferson and Madison. Although the factory produced mainly window glass and bottles, some of their free-blown tablewares have South Jersey and Amelung characteristics (plate 76). The factory moved across the Monongahela River to Greensboro, Pennsylvania, in 1807 and for several decades continued to produce window glass and bottles, along with some free-blown tablewares.

A close runner-up for the distinction of making the first Midwestern glass was the Pittsburgh Glass Works, a factory which, like New Geneva, was also started in 1797 and made its first glass in 1798, a few months after New Geneva. This Pittsburgh glasshouse was founded by General James O'Hara and Major Isaac Craig, two veterans of the Revolutionary Army. It produced mainly window glass and bottles and is significant for being the earliest long-lived glassmaking enterprise in the Midwest, continuing in operation under various firm names until at least 1886.

One of America's great nineteenth-century glass factories was Bakewell's of Pittsburgh. Founded in 1808 as Bakewell and Ensell, the firm name changed so often with changes in partners that collectors have come to refer to it simply as Bakewell's. But whether it was called Bakewell & Page, as in 1811, or Bakewell, Pears and Company, as it became in 1836, there was always a Bakewell in management firmly maintaining the high-quality glass and production standards for which this prestigious company is famous.

Bakewell's was the first successful producer of flint (lead) glass in the Midwest. From the beginning the firm won awards for its fine

77.
American cut glass in Anglo-Irish style was equal to or better than contemporary Anglo-Irish productions. All high-quality lead crystal, probably made by the Bakewell company, Pittsburgh, Pennsylvania, 1815–35. Height of decanter: 26.8 cm. (10½ in.). Corning Museum of Glass, Corning, N.Y.

cut (plate 77) and engraved tableware. It may have been America's first glasshouse to produce cut glass commercially. By 1810 it had made the first cut-glass chandelier produced in the nation. In 1817, filling an order from President Monroe, it became the first American glass factory to make a table service for the White House, and in 1829 was similarly honored by President Jackson.

Bakewell's scored still another first in 1825 when John P. Bakewell received a patent for producing machine-pressed glass furniture knobs. This marked the first step in the machine-pressing of glass, a revolutionary development of glass manufacture that was to become America's single most important nineteenth-century contribution to commercial glass manufacture. By this method, glass could be cheaply made in an endless variety of forms and patterns. The method caught on quickly and within five years many companies were using it.

While Bakewell's and other nineteenth-century glasshouses were bringing fame to the Pittsburgh area (colorplate 25), glass was also being made in eastern Ohio. Among the most important of these early factories were the Zanesville Glass Manufacturing Company (1815 to about 1851), the Mantua Glass Works (1822–29) and a glassworks in Kent (about 1824 to 1834). Although bottles and flasks were the

78.
The lancet-and-leaf-pattern casket (honey dish) and the plates in shells-and-circles pattern with bull's-eye border and Ohio River steamboat pressed in clear glass were Midwestern lacy glass patterns made to rival contemporary New England products. All except the opaque white boat-shaped salt, marked *J. P. Robinson & Son Pittsburgh*, were produced by unidentified Pittsburgh-area factories, 1830–50. Diameter of octagonal plate: 15.5 cm. (6⅛ in.). Corning Museum of Glass, Corning, N.Y.

principal commercial products, free-blown and pattern-molded wares, often in the Stiegel tradition, were made in brilliant green and amber shadings as well as the rarer blues and amethysts, usually in soda-lime glass. Today's collectors are especially interested in the chestnut (shaped) flasks, the rare footed creamers, the sugar bowls with galleried rims and double-domed covers and the more common swirled and ribbed flasks and bottles. In Ohio and other Midwest areas a few sugar bowls, pitchers and salts were produced by blowing the glass into full-size molds having designs taken from cut-glass motifs, a method now known as *blown-three-mold*.

From the late 1820s to the 1850s pressed *lacy glass* made in the Pennsylvania and West Virginia areas competed with that being made in New England. Lacy glass was so called because the designs, often floral and foliate, were combined with a stippled background, giving a lacy appearance to the glassware. Where the first lacy glass was made is still being researched. Factories in New England and the Pittsburgh area, as well as in France (Baccarat) and Belgium (Val-Saint-Lambert), are among those known to have made early pieces. While Midwestern lacy was not produced in as wide a variety of shapes and colors as was its New England counterpart, the Midwestern

79.
Rare Midwestern lacy pane, or panel, pressed in clear colorless glass. The Ohio riverboat design in the center suggests it was intended as a unit for glazing the clerestory of one of the picturesque Ohio steamers. The molded letters *J. & C. Ritchie* spell out the name of the Wheeling factory where the pane was made in the 1830s. Height: 17.8 cm. (7 in.). Smithsonian Institution, National Museum of History and Technology

Colorplate 25.
English influence is apparent in the air-twist and spiral threads in the candlestick stem and the loopings on the vase, contrasting with the pillar-molded (heavy ribbed) pitcher and bar bottle, often called riverboat glass. The pressed-glass compote in petal-and-loop design was made by the Boston & Sandwich Glass Company, Massachusetts. All others are Pittsburgh area and all are mid-nineteenth century. Height of candlestick: 29.5 cm. (11⅝ in.). Corning Museum of Glass, Corning, N.Y.

productions make their own statement and contribute a refreshing local flavor to this popular collector's item (plate 78).

A Midwestern rarity, also found in New England, was the lacy pane, or panel, about seven inches high by five inches wide, which was used primarily as a sidelight for doors or in cupboards. Special designs intended for specific uses, such as glazing the clerestories of riverboats, are especially hard to find and are avidly sought by collectors (plate 79).

Glassmaking in West Virginia got under way about the same time as in the neighboring Ohio and Pittsburgh areas, and productions somewhat paralleled the glass made in these glassmaking centers. The first West Virginia factory, Isaac Duval & Company, Wellsburg (1813 to the 1840s), made fine flint-glass tablewares as well as bottles. The important Wheeling factories included Ritchie & Wheat (1829–?), S. G. Robinson (1830–51) and the South Wheeling Glass Works, founded in 1835. This last factory, which became J. H. Hobbs, Brockunier & Company in 1863 and operated under that name until the 1890s, made one of the greatest contributions to the late nineteenth-century pressed-glass industry. This was a new formula for soda-lime glass, perfected in 1864 by the factory manager, William L. Leighton. Leighton's formula produced a glass nearly as clear and brilliant as the more expensive flint glass and soon replaced this more

expensive glass in the manufacture of better-grade pressed wares.

During the last half of the nineteenth century, thousands of pressed-pattern glass designs were produced by glasshouses from New England to the Midwest. At the Centennial Exposition in 1876, Gillinder & Sons of Philadelphia established a branch factory on the exhibition grounds and sold souvenir pressed-glass pieces. Their Liberty Bell and Westward Ho (then called Pioneer) patterns were especially popular (plate 80).

Midwestern factories also produced an amazing variety of colored glass ranging from solid blues, greens and amethysts to the Wheeling Peach Blow, Mother-of-Pearl Satin, Spangled, Shaded Opalescent (plate 81) and other art glasses of the later decades. Milk white glasses, which varied from opaque and translucent whites to fiery opalescents, were produced in both Midwestern and New England factories, sometimes in similar patterns (plate 82). All types have been longtime favorites with collectors, and there are many reproductions of popular patterns.

The years from about 1810 to 1890 were the period of great expansion for the Midwestern glass industry. At least 130 factories were established in the Ohio, Pennsylvania and West Virginia area. Many of these factories were short-lived, but an amazing number continued for several decades and a few lasted into the twentieth century. In spite of the flourishing conditions in the last half of the nineteenth century, by 1900 only a handful of glasshouses remained in operation.

On November 1, 1899, nineteen glass companies in Ohio, West Virginia, Pennsylvania and Indiana merged to form the National Glass Company. Earlier, on July 1, 1891, eighteen other factories from the same general area had also merged, becoming the United States Glass Company. Both mergers encountered difficulties. The National Glass Company lasted less than three years. The United States Glass Company was reduced to seven or eight companies by 1900 but regained some stability in 1904 and continued in operation through various reorganizations, producing large quantities of both colored and colorless pressed glass. In 1967 it was acquired by Interpace Corporation and is still in operation under this name in Tiffin, Ohio.

After the diminished glassmaking activity at the end of the nineteenth century, the factories still in operation were joined by several new early twentieth-century ventures. Among the hardy nineteenth-century survivors were The Central Glass Company, Wheeling, West Virginia (1863–1939); A. H. Heisey Glass Company, Newark, Ohio (1890s–1953); and The Fostoria Glass Company, Moundsville, West Virginia (1887–present). Some of the lusty twentieth-century newcomers were Imperial Glass Company, Bellaire, Ohio (1901–present); New Martinsville Glass Manufacturing Company (became Viking Glass Company in 1944), New Martinsville, West Virginia (1900–present); and The Fenton Art Glass Company, Williamstown,

80.
Two of the most successful pressed-pattern glass designs were Westward Ho (covered cake dish), first sold under the name Pioneer about 1876, and Classic (pitcher), about 1893, both made by Gillinder & Sons, Philadelphia. The covered compote in Three Face pattern, by Duncan Miller Glass Company, Washington, Pennsylvania, 1880s, is an example of another very popular design. Height of pitcher: 25.4 cm. (10 in.). Corning Museum of Glass, Corning, N.Y.

81.
Shaded Opalescent glass was made by adding bone ash and arsenic to the glass batch. This produced a glass in which a white pattern developed when the pattern-molded object was cooled and immediately reheated during the forming process. Note the white tips on the ruby hobnail vase (right), the white rim and ribs on the butter dish and the Spanish-lace pattern on the center vase. Hobnail vase, Hobbs, Brockunier & Company, Wheeling, West Virginia. Others by unidentified Midwestern factories. Late nineteenth century. Height of center vase: 30.5 cm. (12 in.). Corning Museum of Glass, Corning, N.Y.

82.
Examples of milk white glass include the Atterbury duck, an innovative covered dish, which was a design patented in 1887 by Atterbury & Company, Pittsburgh. The dolphin candlestick, made by New Bedford (1868–69) or Mount Washington Glass Works (1869–90), illustrates another popular design subject. Two contemporary pressed patterns were the sawtooth covered dish by the Boston & Sandwich Glass Company and the caryatid candlestick, patented in 1870 by the New England Glass Company. Height of dolphin candlestick: 16.5 cm. (6½ in.). Corning Museum of Glass, Corning, N.Y.

80

81

82

West Virginia (1905–present). These companies and a number of other Midwestern factories have produced a great variety of blown and pressed ornamental pieces and tablewares in colored and colorless glasses and all have made special types of glass.

New England Salem, Massachusetts, was the site of the third New World glasshouse, a bottle factory established in 1639, which ran until 1643 or perhaps intermittently until 1661. After this moderately productive operation ceased, there were no other significant ventures in New England until the last quarter of the eighteenth century.

New England's first successful glasshouse was a bottle factory, the Pitkin Glassworks, which operated at East Hartford, Connecticut, from 1783 to 1830. While its main productions were common green and black bottles, it is more famous today for two types of flasks, the Pitkin and the figured. The first of these, produced between 1800 and 1830, included pocket bottles and larger flasks that were pattern-molded in vertically ribbed, swirled or broken-swirled-ribbed decorations. The fold just below the neck of the flasks shows they were made by the German half-post method in which most of the flask was covered with a second gather of glass. Although many other factories produced this type of flask during the nineteenth century, its early attribution to the Pitkin glasshouse is so well established that all flasks of this style are now called Pitkin regardless of where or when they were made (plate 83).

About 1815 the Pitkin Glassworks began producing figured (or

83.
Pitkin-type flasks blown in shades of amber glass by the German half-post method. The two broader flasks (second and sixth from left) with broken swirl decoration were made by Midwestern glasshouses. All others made in Connecticut and New Hampshire factories, c. 1800–1830. Height of bottle with stopper: 15.3 cm. (6 in.). Corning Museum of Glass, Corning, N.Y.

historical) flasks blown in full-size molds with relief decorations ranging from sometimes unrecognizable busts of George Washington or Jenny Lind to eagles and cornucopias. From about 1815 to 1840 many other factories also produced figured flasks. Originally made as inexpensive containers for cheap whiskey, they were usually thrown away as soon as they were emptied. However, ever since George S. and Helen McKearin listed 398 figured-flask patterns in their book *American Glass* in 1941, collectors have vied with each other to obtain the surviving flasks—especially those with unusual designs and rare colors (plate 84).

During the nineteenth century, control of glass-factory operations moved away from glamorous entrepreneurs like Stiegel and Amelung to factory managers often dominated by the factory owners. In spite of this trend, from time to time there emerged a personality strong enough to leave a lasting imprint on the development of the glass industry.

Thomas Cains was one of these. This hardy Englishman, sometimes called "the father of the New England flint-glass industry," was employed at the South Boston Flint Glass Works from 1812 to 1819. He then founded his own Phoenix Glassworks in South Boston, which he ran until his death in 1865 at the age of eighty-six. Cains's productions ranged from mold-blown tablewares, inspired by Anglo-Irish cut glass, to delightful free-blown flint-glass productions (plate 85) which established the American trend toward English styles and techniques that has continued to the present day.

84.
Three mold-blown figured (sometimes called historical) flasks made in widely separated areas. The flask portraying Benjamin Franklin was made in Wheeling, West Virginia, c. 1825–30; the General Washington flask was made in the Kensington Glass Works, Philadelphia, 1826–30; and the horse-drawn cart inscribed *Success to the Railroad* was made in Coventry, Connecticut, c. 1825–40. Height of each: about 15.3 cm. (6 in.). Smithsonian Institution, National Museum of History and Technology

85.
Flint (lead) glass free-blown in English traditional styles with applied neck rings on the decanter, horizontal mercurial ring (internal triangular ridge) on the sugar bowl and chain decorations on the pitcher. The coin in the hollow knop in the sugar bowl stem is a George III shilling dated 1816. Probably made by Thomas Cains at the South Boston or Phoenix Glassworks, Boston, 1815–30. Height of sugar bowl: 28 cm. (11 in.). Corning Museum of Glass, Corning, N.Y.

The names Amberina, Pomona, Wild Rose and Agata may not have much meaning to the uninitiated, but to collectors of late nineteenth-century art glass they symbolize the outstanding productions of the New England Glass Company. This famous glasshouse, which operated in East Cambridge, Massachusetts, from 1818 to 1888, might be called New England's answer to Bakewell's. Like the Pittsburgh company's, its early glass included everything from rich-cut tablewares and chandeliers to urinals and breast pumps.

In 1826 Henry Whitney, an official of the company, secured the second American patent for pressed glass. This launched the factory's pressed-glass program, and from the late 1820s to the 1840s its pressed lacy wares compared favorably with those of all competitors (plate 86). During the 1850s cased and stained pieces with cut and engraved designs in Bohemian style became an important production (plate 87). Silvered (mercury) glass was also added about this time and both productions continued to be made well into the 1870s.

The management of the company changed in 1878, as indicated by the name, "New England Glass Works, Wm. L. Libbey & Son, Props." In 1883 production of art glass was begun by Joseph Locke, who had recently come from England, where he had become noted for his cameo-glass copy of the Portland Vase.

The first art glass to be produced by the factory was Amberina, which was patented by Locke in 1883. This was a transparent glass

86.
Pressed lacy tablewares and toys (often called miniatures today) in clear flint glass made in the New England area. The sugar bowl in double-headed-eagle pattern is like the one presented to Mrs. Nikita Khrushchev by the then First Lady, Mrs. John F. Kennedy. Providence Flint Glass Company, Providence, Rhode Island, 1831–32. Height of sugar bowl: 14.5 cm. (5⅜ in.). The plate dates about 1825–30. All others, 1830–40. Corning Museum of Glass, Corning, N.Y.

shading from an amber base to a rich ruby red top (plate 88). Made in a variety of pattern-molded and free-blown styles, it was far more popular at that time than the factory's other art glasses: Pomona, patented in 1885 (colorplate 27); Wild Rose and Plated Amberina, patented in 1886 (colorplate 26); and Agata, patented in 1887.

Declining sales and finally a strike caused the company to close its Massachusetts operation in 1888. Within a few months Edward D. Libbey, the son and surviving owner, moved Locke and a number of other employees to Toledo, Ohio, where he established what became the Libbey Glass Company. In the late nineteenth and early twentieth centuries this firm produced many fine cut and engraved glass pieces (plate 89) and is still operating as the Libbey Products Division of Owens-Illinois, Inc.

Over the years the Boston & Sandwich Glass Company of Sandwich, Massachusetts, has become New England's best-known nineteenth-century glasshouse. It was founded in 1825 by Deming Jarves, who had begun his glassmaking career in 1818 as one of the founders of the New England Glass Company. From 1825 to 1858, under Jarves's guidance, this Cape Cod glasshouse competed successfully with its New England and Midwestern rivals in a wide variety of established glassmaking techniques and pioneered in the mechanical production of pressed glass.

87.
Bohemian-style footed tumblers in clear colorless glass with ruby stained surface. As the inscriptions declare, the engraved decorations depict the State House, Boston (left), and the President's House, Washington. Probably New England Glass Company, East Cambridge, Massachusetts, c. 1860. Height of each: 15.3 cm. (6 in.). Collections of Greenfield Village and the Henry Ford Museum, Dearborn, Mich.

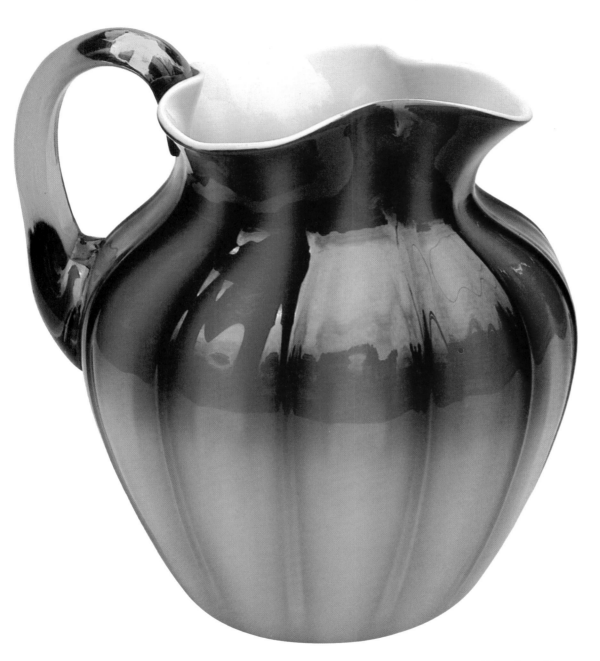

Colorplate 26.
This Plated Amberina pitcher with pattern-molded ribbing and applied handle is one of the rarest American art glasses. New England Glass Company, East Cambridge, Massachusetts, c. 1886. Height: 17.8 cm. (7 in.). Houston Antique Museum, Chattanooga

88

89

88.
Pattern-molded Amberina glass pitchers shaded from amber at the base to ruby red at the top. The glass formula contained a small amount of colloidal gold, which enabled the glassblower to develop the ruby color at the top by cooling and then reheating that portion of the glass during the forming process. New England Glass Company, East Cambridge, Massachusetts, 1880s. Height of pitcher at left: 21.6 cm. (8½ in.). Houston Antique Museum, Chattanooga

89.
Entitled Apotheosis of Transportation, this extremely fine intaglio wheel-engraving on lead-crystal glass was especially designed and produced for the Louisiana Purchase Exhibition, St. Louis, Missouri. Libbey Glass Company, Toledo, Ohio, 1904. Diameter: 31.1 cm. (12¼ in.). Smithsonian Institution, National Museum of History and Technology

90.
Glass banks were often whimsical expressions of individual glassmakers. This rare example is free-blown in light blue glass with white loopings and applied bail handles, chicken finial and rigaree decorations in clear colorless glass. The hollow knop in the stem contains a U.S. half dime dated 1829. Boston & Sandwich Glass Company, Sandwich, Massachusetts, 1830s. Height: 20.4 cm. (8 in.). Chrysler Museum at Norfolk, Norfolk, Va.

90

·During its entire operation the factory made fine hand-blown glass and won awards for its cut and engraved tablewares. Its productions ranged from special dinner services and presentation pieces to such delightful novelties as "bellows bottles" and banks (plate 90). Lamps were also important production items. During the earlier years, whale-oil lamps were made in quantities, either entirely free-blown or with free-blown bowls attached to pressed bases. These were superseded in the 1840s by kerosene and other fluid-burning types, sometimes made in fine ruby and other rich colors often cased with white and decorated with cut patterns in Bohemian styles.

Of even greater importance to the industry than the fine quality and diversity of Sandwich glass was the tremendous impetus which the factory under Jarves's direction gave to the development of machine-pressed glass. His early patents for machine-pressing processes included: 1828 (shape and ornament); 1829 (glass screw on furniture knob); and 1830 (mold for pressing a handled object in one operation). These patents hastened the progress of machine-pressing of glass objects. As might have been expected, pressed wares of all types were a major part of the factory's productions as long as it was in operation (plate 91). The fame of Sandwich lacy glass is too well known to need further elaboration. These ornate tablewares and decorative pieces were introduced in the late 1820s and continued in vogue until the 1850s. Of equal importance to collectors are many other types of pressed designs including dolphin, caryatid and looped-base candlesticks, also made from the 1830s to the 1850s. After the popularity of pressed lacy waned, the factory turned to the less ornate pressed pattern glass. These strong forms, many with wide plain panels and geometric motifs, were made in lively blues, greens, amethysts and yellows.

Blown-three-mold (mentioned earlier and often called BTM) was also one of the earliest types of glass made at Sandwich. Its production paralleled that in other New England and Midwestern factories and included tumblers, pitchers, bowls and decanters all made in a variety of designs, usually with cut-glass motifs. Although the differences of opinion concerning BTM's artistic merits may never be reconciled, Sandwich made some of the most pleasing patterns of this imitation cut glass (colorplate 28).

In the 1870s and 1880s the same economic woes plagued the Boston & Sandwich Glass Company as troubled other New England glass-houses. As with its rival, the New England Glass Company, a strike was the final cause of the factory's closing in 1888.

The Mount Washington Glass Works was the chief competitor of the New England Glass Company in the production of late nineteenth-century art glass. The early years, in South Boston and after the company moved to New Bedford, were beset with management changes and production difficulties. Frederick Shirley, an Englishman,

91.
Cup plates, fashionable from about the 1820s to the 1860s, were used to hold a tea or coffee cup while the beverage was being drunk from the saucer. Left to right: *Cadmus*, so called because it may represent the ship which brought Lafayette to America in 1824; *Henry Clay*, probably issued when Henry Clay was running for President; and *Chancellor Livingston*, the last ship built by Robert Fulton. Boston & Sandwich Glass Company, Sandwich, Massachusetts, 1830s–1840s. Diameters: about 7 to 9 cm. (3 to 3½ in.). Smithsonian Institution, National Museum of History and Technology

92.
Royal Flemish was designed to appeal to late Victorian taste. It was a transparent glass stained and painted with enamels in muted colors and raised gilding, usually in exotic designs such as these vases featuring pseudo coats of arms and Near Eastern scenes. Mount Washington Glass Works, New Bedford, Massachusetts, c. 1890. Height of center vase: 32.4 cm. (12¾ in.). Chrysler Museum at Norfolk, Norfolk, Va.

93.
Venetian-style decanter free-blown in deep purple glass with gold flakes and cased in clear colorless glass. Stopper in clear colorless glass enclosing gold flecks. Union Glass Company, Somerville, Massachusetts, c. 1905. Height: 23 cm. (9 in.). Smithsonian Institution, National Museum of History and Technology

brought new life to the company when he became manager in 1874. He began experimenting with innovative formulas and patented his lava glass in 1878. This glass and some of his other early experimental wares seem to have had little public appeal. Perhaps tempted by Amberina's almost instant success, he brought out a copy of this shaded glass within a year after the New England Glass Company had patented it. This brought instant action from that company, and Shirley narrowly escaped a lawsuit by calling his glass Rose Amber, a name he finally patented in 1886.

Burmese, a translucent glass shaded from a delicate yellow base to a soft rose top (patented in 1885), was Mount Washington's most famous art glass (see colorplate 27). When Burmese was shown in England, Queen Victoria praised it so highly that Thomas Webb & Sons obtained a license to produce it in England under the name Queen's Burmese.

In 1886 Shirley patented Mount Washington Peach Blow, Mother-of-Pearl Satin Glass and the notorious Rose Amber. The ornate Crown Milano, Royal Flemish (plate 92) and Albertine, patented in the 1890s, rounded out Mount Washington's art glass.

In 1894 Mount Washington was purchased by the Pairpoint Manufacturing Company, a silver-plating company located next door. During the next half century this long-lived firm changed management several times, finally becoming the Pairpoint Glass Company in 1957. In 1958, after a year in East Wareham, Massachusetts, it moved to Spain, where it operated sporadically until 1970. In that year it was moved back to Massachusetts, where it is still in operation at Sagamore.

The only New England glass factory in continuous operation from the mid-nineteenth to well into the twentieth century was the Union Glass Company of Somerville, Massachusetts. Early officials of this company, which was founded in 1851, included Amory and Francis Houghton, who left Union in 1863 to run the Brooklyn Flint Glass Works in Brooklyn, New York. In 1868 they moved this factory to Corning, New York, where it has continued as the Corning Glass Works to the present day, always with members of the Houghton family as officials.

Early products of the Union Glass Company were lighting devices and tablewares. After Julian de Cordova became president of the company in 1891, he introduced Art Nouveau jack-in-the-pulpit vases and footed bowls with hooked decorations in Tiffany style. Wares were usually marked *Kew-Blas*, an anagram of W. S. Blake, the factory's manager. A group of tablewares and vases in Venetian style was given to the Smithsonian Institution by Cordova in 1905 (plate 93).

Colorplate 27.
Two popular Victorian art glasses produced by Massachusetts factories were Burmese (three pieces on left), made in bright and matt finishes by the Mount Washington Glass Works, and Pomona (two pieces on right), made by the New England Glass Company. Pieces date from 1885 to 1895. Height of Burmese vase: 26.4 cm. (10⅜ in.). Smithsonian Institution, National Museum of History and Technology

The Empire State   From the mid-eighteenth to the early twentieth century glassmaking in New York State followed the same general pattern of development as that followed in New England and the Midwestern areas. Only about three window-glass and bottle factories were operating in the second half of the eighteenth century. The big increase in glassmaking activity came during the nineteenth century, when about forty companies were in operation at various times. This was followed by a general decline, with a smaller number still running when the century came to an end.

In the first half of the nineteenth century the majority of the New York State factories produced window and bottle glass. Some of these also made fine offhand pieces, often with lily-pad decorations in South Jersey style (colorplate 29). From about midcentury a few flint-glass factories made free-blown cut and engraved glass equal in quality to the Midwestern and New England competition.

C. Dorflinger & Sons was one of the few nineteenth-century flint-glass companies which continued into the twentieth century. Its cut and engraved glass ranked with the best nineteenth- and early twentieth-century productions, and the prestige of this outstanding factory is being reestablished as knowledge of its fine glass becomes more widely available. The factory's founder and guiding genius was Christian Dorflinger, a Frenchman, who had gained his early glassmaking experience at the Compagnie des Cristalleries de Saint-Louis, France, now well known for its paperweights.

Dorflinger's French background is evidenced in many of his productions. A delightful table service made for Mary Todd Lincoln in 1861 (plate 94) and a decanter and glasses in cut glass with engraved seals of the states, made for the Philadelphia Centennial, show the delicacy and elegance often evident in French glassware. Dorflinger's factories operated in Brooklyn, New York (about 1852 and 1858 to about 1863 and perhaps later), and in White Mills, Pennsylvania (about 1866 to the 1920s).

One of the most famous American glass-cutting and engraving establishments was T. G. Hawkes & Company, which operated from 1880 to 1962 in Corning, New York. Although the Hawkes company did not melt its own glass, it represents one of the important areas of the glass industry—those decorating establishments which purchased their glass blanks from various glass factories and decorated them with their own designs. These independent operations ranged from small cutting shops with one or two artisans working in their homes to large companies such as Hawkes, which employed up to four hundred cutters and engravers around the turn of the century.

Thomas Gibbons Hawkes, founder of the company, was a native of Ireland whose family was connected with the Irish glass industry in Waterford. He was also one of the major stockholders in the Steuben Glass Works and was instrumental in bringing Frederick

Colorplate 28.
Blown-three-mold, as it is now called, was a mold-blown glass often having designs taken from nineteenth-century Anglo-Irish cut glass. These pieces show the similarity of New England and Midwestern designs. Pitcher (left), Boston & Sandwich Glass Company; decanter (left) and inkwell, Keene (Marlboro Street) Glassworks, Keene, New Hampshire; decanter (right), Kent, Ohio; sugar bowl and pitcher (right), Midwestern factories. 1815–1830s. Height of decanter (right): 25.5 cm. (10 in.). Corning Museum of Glass, Corning, N.Y.

Colorplate 29.
Two rare free-blown pitchers with applied threading and lily-pad decorations in South Jersey style made by unidentified New York State factories, 1830–50. The pattern-molded sugar bowl with galleried rim was probably produced in Zanesville, Ohio, 1815–30. Height of pitcher (left): 22.4 cm. (8¾ in.). Corning Museum of Glass, Corning, N.Y.

COLORPLATE 28

COLORPLATE 29

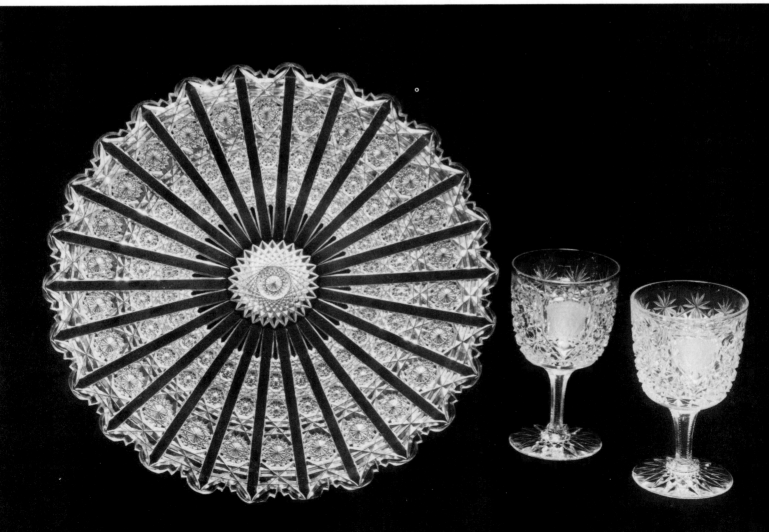

94.
Free-blown compote in lead-crystal glass with cut stem and cut and engraved decorations, including White House insignia. Part of a set ordered by Mary Todd Lincoln for the executive mansion in 1861. Glassworks of Christian Dorflinger, Brooklyn, New York. Height: 22.6 cm. (8⅞ in.). Metropolitan Museum of Art, New York, gift of Kathryn Hait Dorflinger Manchee, 1972

95.
Plate in clear colorless (lead-crystal) glass cut in panel pattern. Goblets in lead-crystal glass cut in Russian pattern and engraved with Presidential crest. T. G. Hawkes & Company, Corning, New York, c. 1882–1900. Diameter of plate: 35.5 cm. (14 in.). Smithsonian Institution, Museum of History and Technology

Carder to Corning to set up the Steuben factory and make blanks for the Hawkes company to decorate.

From its beginnings Hawkes made prestige glass (plate 95), winning the Grand Prize at the Paris Exposition of 1889. The White House began using Hawkes glass when President Cleveland purchased a six-hundred-piece set cut in the Russian pattern in 1885. Presidents Benjamin Harrison and Theodore and Franklin D. Roosevelt continued to use Hawkes glass during their administrations. Other celebrities as diverse as President Díaz of Mexico, Sir Thomas Lipton and Chiang Kai-shek also bought special services. During the "brilliant" period of cut glass, from the 1880s to about 1910, the company was in its heyday and played a major role in making Corning an internationally famous glass center.

Another contributor to Corning's glassmaking reputation was the glassworks of H. P. Sinclaire & Company, which began operating in Corning in 1904 and continued in that city and nearby Bath until 1929. Under the leadership of H. P. Sinclaire, Jr., and other members of the Sinclaire family, its fine hand-blown glass with its distinctive cut and engraved patterns rivaled that of Steuben and other contemporary factories.

Louis Comfort Tiffany (1848–1933), scion of the famous New York family of jewelers, was an established artist as well as a successful interior designer before he became a "gentleman glassmaker." Windows were Tiffany's first essay at glassmaking, starting with a simple bull's-eye semicircular installation in the Church of the Sacred Heart, New York City, in 1876. His best designs were done from the 1880s to about 1910. While Tiffany used most of the traditional techniques in designing and fabricating his windows, he also introduced many innovations such as relief folds molded in the drapery and subtle color effects often composed of many layers of glass. Designs ranging from biblical scenes for churches to idyllic landscapes and still-life arrangements with grapes and corn were installed in dozens of public buildings and private residences.

In his Favrile (hand-wrought) glass, Tiffany achieved the finest in Art Nouveau designs (colorplate 22, see page 84) while exploiting what most glassmakers considered flaws—bubbles, seeds and striae. He also originated many intricate fused and colored combinations (plate 96). His lamps, which varied from the clustered lily shades to the elaborate leaded-glass domes in Wisteria, Apple Blossom and Dragon Fly patterns, came out of the oblivion of the 1930s to attain enormous popularity in the 1960s and 1970s (plate 97). His legacy, an elegant use of a glamorous material, has reestablished Louis Comfort Tiffany as one of the giants of American glassmaking.

A contemporary competitor of Tiffany's was Frederick Carder, a talented Englishman who was a successful designer and an eminent glass technologist with the well-known English glasshouse of Stevens &

96

97

Colorplate 30.
Early Carder Steuben glass (left to right): Red Aurene vase; Gold Aurene jack-in-the-pulpit vase; alabaster vase with Gold Aurene hooked decorations; Gold Aurene vase; Blue Aurene cologne bottle; and Gold Aurene vase with *millefiori* and trailed-leaf decorations. Large Tyrian glass disk with hooked decorations in Gold Aurene. All free-blown at the Steuben Glass Works, Corning, New York, 1905–c. 1916. Diameter of disk: 40.4 cm. (15⅞ in.). Corning Museum of Glass, Corning, N.Y.

96.
Rare paperweight vase of clear colorless glass with floral inclusions in the pedestal base. Marked in script on bottom: *L. C. Tiffany—Favrile 291315.* Tiffany Furnaces, Corona, Long Island, New York, early twentieth century. Height: 19.2 cm. (7½ in.). Cooper-Hewitt Museum, collection of Stanley Siegel, gift of Stanley Siegel

97.
Table lamp with leaded-glass shade in Dragon Fly design and bronze base. Marked in the metal mountings inside the shade: *Tiffany Studios, New York.* Produced at Tiffany Studios, Corona, Long Island, New York, 1900–1905. Height: 56 cm. (22 in.). Cooper-Hewitt Museum, gift of Margaret Carnegie Miller

98.
Rare Intarsia glass vase in which the foliate pattern in black glass, which appears to be a very dark blue because it is so thin, is enclosed between two thin layers of lead-crystal glass. Engraved facsimile signature: *Fred'k Carder*. Designed by Frederick Carder and produced at the Steuben Division, Corning Glass Works, Corning, New York, c. 1930. Height: 19.1 cm. (7½ in.). Collection David L. Williams

Williams before he came to Corning, New York, to found the Steuben Glass Works in 1903. Although Carder did no actual glassblowing, he originated all the glass formulas, designed the glass forms and decorations, kept a firm hand on production and directed sales and advertising. During the nearly three decades he ran the Steuben factory, it produced fine hand-blown glass in a multitude of colors and complicated techniques. Carder's gold and blue Aurene glasses (colorplate 30) rivaled Tiffany's iridescent Favrile productions, and his rare *millefiori*, opalescent and elegant cased ruby, amethyst, blue and green tablewares with high-quality cut and engraved decorations were exhibited in major museums. Although Steuben's productions included many technical triumphs, Carder considered Intarsia glass his greatest technical achievement. This glass was produced experimentally about 1917 and intermittently in very limited quantities until about 1931. Its final form had a design in a thin layer of blue, bluish black, amethyst or green enclosed between two thin layers of crystal (plate 98). Fewer than fifty of these rare pieces are known, and all except a few have an engraved facsimile signature reading, "Fred'k Carder."

During World War I the factory was declared a nonessential industry and was unable to purchase glassmaking materials. This resulted in its purchase by Corning Glass Works and from then until 1933 it operated as the Steuben Division of Corning Glass Works. In 1932 Carder was appointed art director of the Corning Glass Works. From then until he retired in 1959, at the age of ninety-six, he designed for that company and pursued his experimentations with difficult glassmaking techniques in his studio-office. His greatest achievement during these years was the development of the *cire perdue* (lost wax) process for casting glass, a technique which he carried to a greater degree of perfection than anyone had previously attained (plate 99). In producing these pieces Carder made the wax model, poured the ceramic mold and melted the glass in his studio furnace. The most intricate of these pieces, which he called Diatreta, symbolize his success in this involved technique. During his nearly eighty years in artistic glass production, Carder used, adapted or evolved more glassmaking techniques than any other American glassmaker up to that time.

Since 1933 Steuben Glass, under the direction of Arthur A. Houghton, Jr. (1933–73), and Thomas S. Buechner (1973–   ), has produced hand-blown lead-crystal glass of the finest quality. Many of these prestige pieces, enhanced with superb wheel-engravings, have been selected as presentation pieces and gifts for heads of state and other dignitaries. The Corning Glass Works and Steuben Glass maintain a Glass Center in Corning, New York, where visitors can see Steuben glass being made. This complex also contains the Corning Museum of Glass, one of the finest museums of its kind. Its exhibition galleries show outstanding examples illustrating all the important historical eras and technical and artistic glassmaking achievements.

The Twentieth Century   After the decline in the industry toward the end of the nineteenth century, American glassmaking revived as the twentieth century advanced, eventually becoming one of the country's leading industries. A 1977 listing shows 419 glass factories located in 39 states, with branches of the giant combines such as Corning Glass Works, Owens-Illinois and PPG Industries in many foreign countries.

A 1960s movement called Studio Glass is bringing exciting developments to hand-blown glass production. Dominick Labino and Harvey Littleton pioneered in this movement with the backing of Otto Wittmann, then director of the Toledo Museum of Art. Their concept was to bring recognition to the actual producer of the glass object— the glassblower. In traditional factory production, the glassblower is anonymous. The credit for the finished glass goes to the factory or,

99.
Cire perdue (lost wax) casting of figure with lyre in clear colorless lead glass with satin finish. Designed and cast by Frederick Carder. Corning Glass Works, Corning, New York, 1930s. Height: about 20.5 cm. (8 in.). Corning Museum of Glass, Corning, N.Y.

in some cases, to the designer. In the Studio Glass Movement the glass-maker designs the productions, melts the glass and fabricates the pieces from the fire to the annealing kiln.

Starting with fewer than a dozen participants in 1962, this American movement had grown by the mid-1970s to include more than three hundred glassmakers. At least one hundred colleges and technical schools have added glassmaking instruction to their programs. The Studio Glass Movement has spread to Europe, Australia and Japan and augurs well for the future of hand-blown glass. The vases, paper-weights and other decorative objects made by the talented glassmakers of the movement have already become a fascinating new area for col-lectors.

5 Advice for Glass Collectors

Interest in collecting glass has increased rapidly since the 1930s. Whether you collect for pleasure, profit or a combination of these motives, there are some helpful procedures which have successfully guided collectors of ornamental and high-quality useful wares in acquiring their treasures.

It is a temptation, especially at first, to collect everything that strikes one's fancy. While no one will criticize a person who wants to amass a variety of objects, collectors soon find it best to specialize. To assist in choosing a specialty it is advisable to study collections and related reference material. Go where you can see glass pieces at close range and, better still, touch them. By handling the glass you can learn to sense weight, feel surface textures, test the resonance and see pontil marks and mold seams. By noting these and other identifying characteristics you can make better judgments concerning origins, datings and the quality of the glass. Opportunities to handle and study glass are provided by seminars, workshops, study groups and shops. Reliable dealers are often excellent authorities in their fields. They can be of great assistance in locating and identifying glass pieces for collectors. Moreover, they will usually provide a written guarantee of the authenticity of your purchase.

There are three main factors which determine the value of most ornamental and useful glass objects: rarity, technical excellence and beauty. Of these, rarity seems to be the major factor in determining the monetary value.

A quick value gauge is the price guide. This is both a good and a bad instrument. It should be remembered that price guides are just that, and simply reflect the knowledge of the authors at the time of printing. They may apply more accurately in one area of the country than in another. The better authorities recognize their limitations and very often do not quote prices on very rare or unusual objects.

Beginning collectors are often surprised to learn that many glass pieces have no factory markings. Prior to the late nineteenth century, virtually all factory-produced glass, whether free-blown, mold-blown or pressed, was unmarked. Since that time some factories have marked their wares.

In deciding whether or not to purchase an object, a basic rule is to be sure it is something you admire and want. If it is, and you feel it is worth the price, buy it. Even if it turns out to be less valuable than you thought or not as rare as you hoped, you will probably get your money's worth in the pleasure of ownership or in learning from your mistake. Collectors always develop their own methods and preferences for acquiring pieces. Some like auctions, others prefer to haunt shops and flea markets or seek out private sales. Whatever course you pursue, do not overlook the basic rule in collecting—buy something you will enjoy.

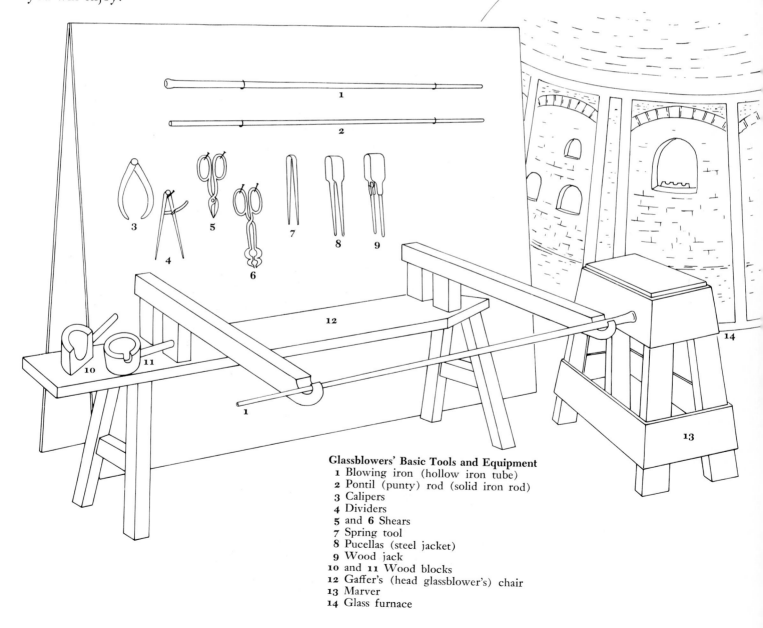

Glassblowers' Basic Tools and Equipment
  1 Blowing iron (hollow iron tube)
  2 Pontil (punty) rod (solid iron rod)
  3 Calipers
  4 Dividers
  5 and 6 Shears
  7 Spring tool
  8 Pucellas (steel jacket)
  9 Wood jack
  10 and 11 Wood blocks
  12 Gaffer's (head glassblower's) chair
  13 Marver
  14 Glass furnace

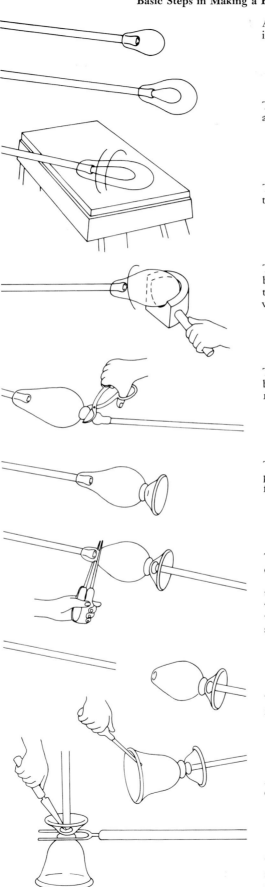

A gather of hot glass is attached to the blowing iron.

The gather is expanded slightly by blowing it into a bubble called a parison.

The parison is partially shaped by rolling it on the marver (a process called marvering).

The parison is expanded by blowing it into a bubble nearly the size of the vase and shaped by tooling, including rounding the bottom in a wooden block.

The button stem is applied to the base of the bubble from a gather of molten glass on the pontil rod and cut off and shaped with shears.

The gather for the foot (base) is applied from the pontil rod in the same way and tooled into the flared base shape.

The pontil rod, having a small gather of hot glass on the end, is attached to the center of the base (a process called sticking up). Then, where the top is attached to the blowing iron, it is scored with the pucellas, which have been dipped in water, causing the glass to crack at the indentation and break away from the blowing iron.

The vase, now firmly attached to the pontil rod, is broken away from the blowing iron.

After reheating, the top of the vase is flared out, completing the form.

The vase is broken from the pontil rod (leaving a scar called the pontil mark) and transferred to the annealing oven.

Glossary

acid-etched, a glass decoration in which a design in wax resist protects part of the glass surface. The unprotected area is eaten away by hydrofluoric acid, leaving the design in relief.

annealing, controlled cooling of glass objects to avoid strains which would cause spontaneous breakage. This cooling is done in an annealing oven called a *kiln* or a *lehr*. The temperature of the newly formed glass is reduced slowly from just below the softening point to about room temperature.

"at the fire," the forming and decorating processes done in the blowing room at or near the glass furnace.

batch, the mixture of sand, soda, lime and other ingredients of the glass formula which are melted to produce glass.

blank, undecorated glass object, usually made and designed for cut, engraved, acid-etched or other decoration to be done at the factory or by outside shops or artisans.

blowing iron (blowpipe), an iron tube usually about 3½ to 4½ feet long and tapering from about 1½ to ½ inch in diameter. The smaller end is rounded slightly to fit the glassblower's mouth, and the larger end bulges slightly to help hold the *gather* of molten glass.

casing, covering a *parison* with one or more layers of hot glass, usually of a different color.

crackle, a decorative effect in which the *parison* is plunged into water, causing the hot glass to crack in a network pattern. The parison is quickly reheated, which fuses the glass but leaves the crackled pattern. A variation of this process used by Venetian glassmakers and others is called ice glass.

crizzle, a fine network of lines in glass caused by an imbalance in the glass formula. This is an indication of "sick" glass. If the imbalance is extreme, the glass will eventually disintegrate into powder.

crown glass, window glass made by flaring a glass bubble into a disk by centrifugal force. This process leaves a bull's-eye in the center where the *pontil rod* was attached.

cullet, broken glass.

dragged decoration, see *hooked decoration*.

flint glass, a term now used almost synonymously with lead glass. It originated in England when flint pebbles were ground to provide silica in the glass batch.

free-blown, all or part of a glass object fashioned by the glassblower "offhand" (primarily without the use of molds).

gaffer, the head glassblower in the group of workers forming a *shop*, one of the working units in the blowing room.

gather, the mass of molten glass gathered or dipped from the glass pot on the end of the *blowing iron* by the glassblower.

German half-post method, a process in which the lower portion of a flask or other object is dipped into the glass pot and covered with a second *gather* of glass, leaving a ring about one or two inches below the top, where the second gather ends.

hooked decoration, a decoration in which trailings or threadings of hot glass are applied to a glass object and pulled up and down or in swirls with a hooked tool. Also called *dragged decoration*.

kiln, an oven used for *annealing* glass objects.

lehr, an *annealing* oven.

lily pad, a decoration in which a layer of glass is applied to the lower part of an object and tooled upward into a form somewhat resembling a lily pad.

marver, a smooth iron or stone plate or table used by the glassblower to shape the *parison* and for other forming processes.

mercurial ring, an internal triangular ridge made by indenting a ring in the hot glass and tooling and melting the indentation back together so that the outer surface is smooth and the ring projects on the inside. Used in America by Thomas Cains of Boston.

merese, a button or wafer of glass used to connect parts of hand-blown stems of goblets and other stemmed pieces.

parison, the hot glass *gather* after it has been partly inflated and shaped by the glassblower.

pincered or *pinched*, a decoration shaped with pincers, while the glass is hot, into a fin, a notch or other ornamental form.

pontil (or *punty*) *mark*, the scar left on the bottom of a piece of hand-blown glass when the *pontil rod* is broken away.

pontil (or *punty*) *rod*, a solid iron rod about the same size as the *blowing iron* (usually smaller in diameter), which is dipped in the molten glass and stuck to the base of hot glass objects to enable the glassworker to finish the top, apply handles and perform other decorative and finishing processes.

prunt, a blob or dab of hot glass applied to the surface of a hot glass piece as a decorative motif. It is sometimes shaped into a raspberry, a mask (human face or lion) or other form by pushing into it a metal mold having the design in reverse, in the same way a seal is impressed in sealing wax.

rigaree, applied glass ribs or bands tooled with horizontal indentations.

shop, a working unit in the blowing room usually composed of from three to six workers: the *gaffer* (head of the shop), servitor (chief assistant), blower, bit gatherer, sticker-up and taker-in (worker who takes the finished ware to the *lehr*).

threading, threads of glass applied to the surface of a glass piece as decoration.

tooling, applied surface decorations including *threading*, *rigaree*, *hooked* and many other manipulations of these trailed and shaped ornamentations. Often called tooled decorations.

trailing, any applied decoration in which the motif is trailed or threaded on the surface of a glass object.

Reading and Reference

General

CORNING MUSEUM OF GLASS. *Glass from the Corning Museum of Glass: A Guide to the Collections.* Rev. ed. Corning, N.Y.: Corning Museum of Glass, 1974.

ELVILLE, E. M. *The Collector's Dictionary of Glass.* New York: Tudor Publishing Co., 1971.

HARDEN, D. B.; K. S. PAINTER; R. H. PINDER-WILSON; AND HUGH TAIT. *Masterpieces of Glass.* London: British Museum, 1968. Exhibition catalogue.

HONEY, W. B. *Glass: A Handbook for the Study of Glass Vessels of All Periods and Countries and a Guide to the Museum Collection.* London: Victoria and Albert Museum, 1946.

NEWMAN, HAROLD. *An Illustrated Dictionary of Glass.* New York: Thames and Hudson, 1978.

PELLATT, APSLEY. *Curiosities of Glass Making.* London: David Bogue, 1849.

POLAK, ADA. *Glass: Its Tradition and Its Makers.* New York: G. P. Putnam's Sons, 1975.

VOSE, RUTH HURST. *The Connoisseur Illustrated Guides: Glass.* New York: Hearst Books, 1976.

American Glass

HUNTER, FREDERICK W. *Stiegel Glass.* 1914. Reprint. New York: Dover Publications, 1966.

INNES, LOWELL. *Pittsburgh Glass 1797–1891: A History and Guide for Collectors.* Boston: Houghton Mifflin Co., 1976.

KNITTLE, RHEA MANSFIELD. *Early American Glass.* 1927. Reprint. Garden City, N.Y.: Garden City Publishing Co., 1948.

LEE, RUTH WEBB. *Early American Pressed Glass.* 30th ed. Northboro, Mass.: the author, 1949.

MCKEARIN, GEORGE S. AND HELEN. *American Glass.* New York: Crown Publishers, 1941.

———. *Two Hundred Years of American Blown Glass.* Rev. ed. New York: Crown Publishers, 1966.

MCKEARIN, HELEN, AND KENNETH M. WILSON. *American Bottles and Flasks and Their Ancestry.* New York: Crown Publishers, 1978.

REVI, ALBERT CHRISTIAN. *American Cut and Engraved Glass.* Camden, N.J.: Thomas Nelson and Sons, 1965.

———. *American Pressed Glass and Figure Bottles.* Camden, N.J.: Thomas Nelson and Sons, 1964.

WATKINS, LURA WOODSIDE. *American Glass and Glassmaking.* New York: Chanticleer Press, 1950.

———. *Cambridge Glass, 1818–1888: The Story of the New England Glass Company.* Boston: Little, Brown and Co., 1953.

WILSON, KENNETH M. *New England Glass and Glassmaking.* New York: Thomas Y. Crowell Co., 1972.

English and Irish Glass

ANGUS-BUTTERWORTH, L. M. *British Table and Ornamental Glass.* New York: Arco Publishing Co., 1962.

ASH, DOUGLAS. *How to Identify English Drinking Glasses and Decanters, 1680–1830.* London: G. Bell, 1962.

———, ED. *Dictionary of British Antique Glass.* Levittown, N.Y.: Transatlantic Arts, 1976.

DAVIS, DEREK C. *English and Irish Antique Glass.* New York: Frederick A. Praeger, 1965.

ELVILLE, E. M. *English Tableglass.* Rev. ed. New York: Taplinger Publishing Co., 1963.

GUTTERY, D. R. *From Broad Glass to Cut Crystal: A History of the Stourbridge Glass Industry.* New York: Arco Publishing Co., 1962.

WAKEFIELD, HUGH. *Nineteenth-Century British Glass.* New York: Thomas Yoseloff, 1962.

WARREN, PHELPS. *Irish Glass: The Age of Exuberance.* London and Salem, N.H.: Faber & Faber, 1970.

WESTROPP, M. S. DUDLEY. *Irish Glass: An Account of Glassmaking in Ireland from the XVIth Century to the Present Day.* London: H. Jenkins, 1920.

Continental Glass

BUCKLEY, WILFRED. *European Glass.* Boston: Houghton Mifflin Co., 1926.

FROTHINGHAM, ALICE WILSON. *Spanish Glass.* New York: Hispanic Society of America, 1964.

MARIACHER, GIOVANNI. *Italian Blown Glass: From Ancient Rome to Venice.* Translated by Michael Bullock and Johanna Capra. New York: McGraw-Hill Book Co., 1961.

STEENBERG, ELISA. *Swedish Glass.* Translated by Lillian Ollén. New York: M. Barrows and Co., 1950.

VON SALDERN, AXEL. *German Enameled Glass.* New York: Crown Publishers, 1971.

Nineteenth- and Twentieth-Century Glass

AMAYA, MARIO. *Tiffany Glass.* New York: Walker and Co., 1968.

BEARD, GEOFFREY W. *International Modern Glass.* New York: Charles Scribner's Sons, 1978.

———. *Nineteenth-Century Cameo Glass.* Newport, Monmouthshire, Wales: Ceramic Book Co., 1956.

GARDNER, PAUL V. *The Glass of Frederick Carder.* New York: Crown Publishers, 1971.

GROVER, RAY AND LEE. *Art Glass Nouveau.* Rutland, Vt.: Charles E. Tuttle Co., 1967.

KOCH, ROBERT. *Louis C. Tiffany, Rebel in Glass.* 2d ed. New York: Crown Publishers, 1966.

———. *Louis C. Tiffany's Glass, Bronzes and Lamps: A Complete Collector's Guide.* New York: Crown Publishers, 1971.

LEE, RUTH WEBB. *Nineteenth-Century Art Glass.* New York: William Morrow and Co., 1952.

MCKEAN, HUGH. *The "Lost" Treasures of Louis Comfort Tiffany.* New York: Doubleday and Co., forthcoming.

POLAK, ADA. *Modern Glass.* New York: Thomas Yoseloff, 1962.

REVI, ALBERT CHRISTIAN. *Nineteenth-Century Glass: Its Genesis and Development.* 2d ed. Camden, N.J.: Thomas Nelson and Sons, 1967.

Specialties

CONNICK, CHARLES J. *Adventures in Light and Color: An Introduction to the Stained Glass Craft.* New York: Random House, 1937.

HOLLISTER, PAUL M. *The Encyclopedia of Glass Paperweights.* New York: Clarkson N. Potter, 1969.

KAMM, MINNIE WATSON. *Two Hundred Pattern Glass Pitchers.* Watkins Glen, N.Y.: Century House, 1968.

LEE, RUTH WEBB. *Antique Fakes and Reproductions.* Enl. and rev. ed. Northboro, Mass.: the author, 1950.

———. *Sandwich Glass.* 4th ed. Northboro, Mass.: the author, 1947.

———. *Victorian Glass.* Northboro, Mass.: the author, 1944.

Periodicals

Journal of Glass Studies. Corning, N.Y.: Corning Museum of Glass. Published annually since 1959. Contains specialized articles by international authorities on a wide variety of glass.

Some Public Collections of Glass

UNITED STATES

Chattanooga, Tenn.:	Houston Antique Museum
Cincinnati, Ohio:	Cincinnati Art Museum
Columbus, Ohio:	Ohio Historical Center
Corning, N.Y.:	The Corning Museum of Glass
Dearborn, Mich.:	Greenfield Village and Henry Ford Museum
Millville, N.J.:	Museum of Glass, Wheaton Historical Association
Neenah, Wis.:	John Nelson Bergstrom Art Center and Museum
Newark, N.J.:	The Newark Museum
New York City:	The Brooklyn Museum
	Cooper-Hewitt Museum, the Smithsonian Institution's National Museum of Design
	Hispanic Society of America
	The Metropolitan Museum of Art
Norfolk, Va.:	Chrysler Museum at Norfolk
Philadelphia:	Philadelphia Museum of Art
Toledo, Ohio:	The Toledo Museum of Art
Washington, D.C.:	Hillwood
	Smithsonian Institution
	National Collection of Fine Arts
	National Museum of History and Technology

OTHER

Cambridge, England:	Fitzwilliam Museum
Cologne:	Römisch-Germanisches Museum
London:	British Museum
	Victoria and Albert Museum
Orrefors, Sweden:	Orrefors Glass Museum
St. Helens, Lancashire, England:	Pilkington Glass Museum
Toronto:	Royal Ontario Museum

Index

Numbers in *italics* indicate pages on which black-and-white illustrations appear.
Numbers in **boldface** indicate pages on which colorplates appear.

Acknowledgments

Among my friends and colleagues without whose generous help and scholarship this book would not have been possible are Philip W. Bishop, Robert H. Brill, Wendy Evans, Nathan L. Ferris, Sidney M. Goldstein, Imogene and William P. Hudson, Paul N. Perrot and Kenneth M. Wilson. Their critical readings and literary assistance were invaluable in the preparation of my manuscript. I am also greatly indebted to Sheila M. Alexander, Jewell S. Dulaney, Brenda Gilchrist, Marilyn Hilton, Joan Hoffman, Peter Kaellgren, Dwight Lanmon, Lisa Little, David McFadden, Nancy O. Merrill, Jon Meyer, Jennifer M. Oka, Arlene Palmer, Priscilla Price, Peter Rath, Christian Rohlfing, Lucien R. Rossignol, Barbara Schnitzer, Paul Stankard and Lisa Taylor. In addition, I wish to express my appreciation to the private collectors and the staff members of museums who provided photographs and other material for this book. To these fine friends and the many others who assisted me in so many ways, my most sincere thanks.

PAUL V. GARDNER

Cooper-Hewitt staff members have been responsible for the following contributions to the series: concept, Lisa Taylor; administration, John Dobkin and Christian Rohlfing; coordination, Pamela Theodoredis. In addition, valuable help has been provided by S. Dillon Ripley, Joseph Bonsignore, Susan Hamilton and Robert W. Mason of the Smithsonian Institution, as well as by the late Warren Lynch, Gloria Norris and Edward E. Fitzgerald of Book-of-the-Month Club, Inc.

Credits

Courtesy of the Trustees of the British Museum: 4, 5, 15, 22, 26, 27. Chrysler Museum at Norfolk: 90, 92. Cooper-Hewitt Museum: 9, 19, 45, 65, 68–70 and color 18 (Helga Photo Studio, Inc.); blowing-room interiors on pages 8 and 10, 35, 40, 43, 97 and color *frontispiece*, 10, 19, 22 (David Allison); 46 (George D. Cowdery); *endpapers*, 96 (Scott Hyde). The Corning Museum of Glass, Corning, N.Y.: 7, 13, 14, 17, 18, 20, 21, 25, 28, 29, 31, 33, 34, 38, 39, 42, 51, 52, 54, 58, 77, 78, 80–83, 85, 86, 98, 99; color 1–4, 6–9, 11–14, 16, 17, 20, 21, 23–25, 28–30 (Raymond F. Errett). Fitzwilliam Museum, Cambridge, England: 59, 61, 62, 64, 66. Collections of Greenfield Village and the Henry Ford Museum, Dearborn, Mich.: 87. Hillwood, Washington, D.C.: 56 (James R. Dunlop). Hispanic Society of America, New York: 48, 49, 53. Houston Antique Museum, Chattanooga: 88 and color 26 (Harold Haven). The Metropolitan Museum of Art, New York: 1, 50, 74, 94; color 5, 15. Rheinisches Bildarchiv Kölnisches Stadtmuseum, Cologne: 8. Courtesy of the Royal Ontario Museum, Toronto, Canada: 32, 71. Smithsonian Institution, National Collection of Fine Arts, Washington, D.C.: 2, 3, 73. Smithsonian Institution (National Museum of History and Technology): 6, 10–12, 16, 30, 36, 37, 44, 47, 55, 57, 60, 63, 67, 72, 75, 76, 79, 84, 89, 91, 93, 95; color 27 (Alfred F. Harrell). Victoria and Albert Museum, Crown Copyright: 23, 24, 41.

DESIGN ASSISTANT: Dolly Carr

LINE DRAWINGS: Judy Skorpil